Daphne Odjig

FOUR DECADES OF PRINTS

Daphne Odjig: Four Decades of Prints

FOREWORD Jann LM Bailey

ESSAY Morgan Wood

Kamloops Art Gallery, Kamloops, British Columbia

If my work as an artist has somehow helped to open doors between our people and the non-Native community, then I am glad. I am even more deeply pleased if it has helped to encourage the young people that have followed our generation to express their pride in our heritage more openly, more joyfully than I would have ever dared to think possible.

DAPHNE ODJIG

Daphne Odjig, quoted in Bob Boyer and Carol Podedworny, *Odjig: The Art of Daphne Odjig 1960–2000* (Toronto: Key Porter Books, 2001) 78.

Foreword

I had the privilege of first meeting Daphne Odjig and her husband, Chester Beavon, in the late 1980s when I traveled a short distance from Kamloops to their magnificent home on the shores of Shuswap Lake. I came away from that day, like many others had before me, with a sense of enchantment in having shared an afternoon with this remarkable and generous woman.

I had been aware of Daphne Odjig and her work for many years prior to our meeting on that warm, extraordinary afternoon, but talking to her about her art and life gave me the incentive to build for the Kamloops Art Gallery the largest public collection of Odjig's print works in Canada.

Daphne Odjig was born and raised on the Wikwemikong Reserve on Manitoulin Island, Ontario. The oldest of four surviving children of Dominic Odjig, a member of the Pottawatomi nation, and Joyce Peacy, an English war bride, Daphne moved with her siblings to her grandmother's house after the death of her mother. Here, her first encounter with prejudice caused her to conceal her First Nations identity for many years.

With her sister Winnie, Daphne moved to Toronto during World War II where she met and married Paul Somerville in 1945. The couple moved that same year to British Columbia, where Somerville encouraged his young bride to explore her deep-rooted interest in art, an interest that began while drawing and painting with her grandfather Jonas Odjig, a tombstone carver by trade. Balancing her self-taught interest in art with the care of her baby son, Stanley, Odjig continued to study the work of Emily Carr and others and to re-explore her Native roots.

Tragically, Paul Somerville died in a car accident in 1960, and Daphne immersed herself in her work to escape the loneliness. She often painted throughout the night and began to experiment with her style and technique while at the same time managing the couple's strawberry farm in order to survive.

In 1963 Daphne married Chester Beavon, a community development officer with the Manitoba government, and the couple moved from B.C. to Manitoba at a time when a number of now well-known First Nations artists were beginning to explore their cultural heritage. As Odjig continued to work and explore her personal style, her first solo exhibition took place in 1967 at the Lakehead Art Centre, Port Arthur, Ontario. By the early 1970s her work had acquired international attention with exhibitions in the USA, Europe, and Japan.

This was an intense time for Odjig: she created the largest number of prints in any given period, opened her own gallery, stood up for Native art, and accepted and completed several major commissions. During this time she also completed an outstanding series of prints depicting the stories and beliefs of Aboriginal people on Manitoulin Island, a series of erotic images to illustrate the book *Tales from the Smokehouse*, and the *Jerusalem Series* prints, for which she traveled to Israel to research.

Daphne and Chester moved from Winnipeg to the Shuswap in 1976. After more than six busy years operating Odjig Indian Prints of Canada and the Warehouse Gallery, with Daphne producing her own work, organizing many group and solo exhibitions — of her own work and the works of Jackson Beardy, Alex Janvier, Norval Morrisseau, Carl Ray, Eddy Cobiness and Joseph Sanchez — and being the unofficial ambassador of First Nations culture within Canada, they wanted a more relaxed pace so they could enjoy life and Daphne could work solely on her own art. It was a move that came on the heels of completing work on a series of prints commissioned by El Al Airlines the previous year, on the Holy Land, titled the *Jerusalem Series*. This remarkable body of work with its use of contrasting primary colours, black form lines, arcs, and curvilinear lines became autobiographical in nature, moving Odjig's work away from earlier representations of Native legends to a more personal interpretation of life.

Throughout the late 1970s, the 1980s and 1990s, Odjig continued to work in several mediums — painting, drawing, collage, and printmaking — and to organize a number of group and solo exhibitions of her work. Prints created during this time include the *Pow Wow Series* (1977), *Motherhood Series* (1979), *Grandfather Series* (1980), *Childhood Memories Series* (1981), *Love Suite* (1981), *Prayer Series* (1983), and the *Love Series* (1992). After 1983, Odjig took a hiatus from printmaking until 1992 when she produced the *Love Series* and generously agreed to produce the serigraph *Enfolding* for the Kamloops Art Gallery's Collecting Canadian Art program.

In 1999 Daphne and Chester moved from their home on Shuswap Lake to the city of Penticton. Since then, Odjig has produced only a few works, including the two serigraphs, *And Some Watch the Sunset* (2001) and *In Tune With the Infinite* (2004), in this exhibition.

Daphne Odjig: Four Decades of Prints brings together 95 works that Odjig created during the past forty years. It is an exhibition that, for the first time, comprehensively celebrates one significant aspect of the artist's life work — printmaking — and provides viewers with the unique opportunity to share in and celebrate Aboriginal cultural heritage through the eyes of one of Canada's most remarkable artists.

Daphne Odjig's prints are representative of the artist's mature work, as she had already been through many experimental phases when she began her interest in printmaking in the late 1960s and early 1970s.[1] To a great extent, Odjig's prints are influenced by her mural works, which were created on large surfaces with bold, colourful imagery. Her first mural was for the Peguis High School in Hodgson, Manitoba, in 1971.[2] The second mural commission, *Creation of the World*, was for Winnipeg's Manitoba Museum of Man and Nature in 1972. Her most well-known mural work was completed in 1978 for the National Museum of Man in Ottawa, Ontario (now the Canadian Museum of Civilization in Gatineau, Quebec).[3] The mural is 8 feet high by 27 feet wide and, as its title implies, articulates Odjig's view of *The Indian in Transition*.

From her first unlimited reproductions in 1968 to her most recent serigraphs, Daphne frequently uses her original paintings and drawings as the basis for the prints. This reproduction-from-original approach to printmaking, while unorthodox, has led to a remarkable body of work. Daphne is steadfast in using this approach, and since her initial experimentation with reproductions in the late 1960s all her prints have been limited edition serigraphs and a few lithographs. For many, her approach is welcome, as it makes her well-known and much-admired images attainable by collectors of modest means.

I would like to thank Daphne Odjig for her friendship, dedication, and generosity in organizing this exhibition, and for assisting the Kamloops Art Gallery in acquiring the largest collection of her print works in Canada. I would also like to thank Chester Beavon for his support of this project, and his good humour.

It is an honour for our regional gallery to undertake the organization of such an important exhibition and to tour it across Canada for others to enjoy. As with any major exhibition, a number of people have assisted with the development and organization of this show over the last year and a half. I would like to thank Geraldine Parent, who worked with the Kamloops Art Gallery staff on the initial research to locate works for this exhibition. I would also like to thank Daphne's son, Stanley Somerville, as well as Grace Brown of Hampton Gallery in Kamloops and Phillip Gevik of Gevik Gallery in Toronto for their assistance in locating or loaning works for this exhibition. Works have also been borrowed from a number of public institutions and private collectors, and I would like to thank them for loaning works to assist with the realization of this project: the Canadian Museum of Civilization, Simon Fraser University Art Gallery, The Winnipeg Art Gallery, Dave Barron, Winnie Christian, and Linda McMillan.

Morgan Wood has produced a catalogue essay that underpins the importance of Daphne's work and highlights the significant contribution Daphne Odjig has made to Canadian art. Morgan, juggling a teaching career at the University of Manitoba with trips to B.C. to meet and interview Odjig and visit the Kamloops Art Gallery to view the work, has been a pleasure to work with.

My continued admiration is extended to the staff of the Kamloops Art Gallery, who are as passionate about this project as I am. I would like to thank everyone on staff, especially Trish Keegan, Erin Moen, Jen Budney, Vaughn Warren, Kim Galloway, James Gordon, Patti Procknow, and Wendy Lysak for their ideas, enthusiasm, and involvement with every aspect of this exhibition.

Along with the Board of Trustees, I would like to acknowledge and thank those who have been so generous in their support of the Kamloops Art Gallery and sponsorship of this exhibition: British Columbia Lottery Corporation, Hampton Gallery, and Simmons, Black & Emsland Insurance Services. In addition, the exhibition and publication are generously supported by the Canada Council for the Arts, the Department of Canadian Heritage, the City of Kamloops, and the British Columbia Arts Council. Our sincere and continued appreciation is extended for this financial assistance.

Jann LM Bailey
Executive Director, Kamloops Art Gallery

Endnotes

1. Daphne Odjig in conversation with the author, April 6, 2005: "Chester and I were in Northern Manitoba and the situation was very sad. The community had been uprooted and I felt I needed to sketch these changes and the people. I called it my series of the North. I was asked by others to reproduce these drawings, which I did, and I started to sell them. When we moved to Winnipeg, printmaker Bill Lobchuck asked me if I thought about making limited editions."

2. Daphne Odjig: "I have to give credit to Bernard Polly, Head of the Art Department at the University of Brandon, Manitoba, who showed me how to create these murals. He came all the way from Brandon to help me."

3. *The Indian in Transition* was commissioned in 1974 by National Museum of Man Director William Taylor.

Daphne Odjig

by Morgan Wood

DUBBED "PICASSO'S GRANDMOTHER" BY THE ARTIST NORVAL MORRISSEAU, DAPHNE Odjig has long been considered one of Canada's artistic geniuses and a national treasure. Co-founder of what has been called the "Indian," "Native" or "Second" Group of Seven — a group of Aboriginal artists who, in the 1970s, originated the distinct Woodland style of painting and printmaking — Odjig possesses a unique visual style consisting of organic shapes and strong lines. This style finds its roots in traditional Aboriginal imagery and culture, yet it is also remarkably innovative. Odjig is equally known for her grace, wisdom, and strength, and for her encouragement of Aboriginal people to pursue their dreams. Possessing four honorary doctoral degrees, she particularly encourages education. Indeed, she explains her pursuit of images through art as a form of education itself:

> Knowledge and cultures evolve and grow. Our goal, as I see it, is to open our eyes to see, unplug our ears to hear, to find new ways, share new ideas, open the door to change, and grow and grow and grow.[1]

Odjig was born in 1919 at Wikwemikong,[2] Manitoulin Island,[3] of mixed Pottawatomi and English heritage. She grew up in a loving home, but at an early age contracted rheumatic fever and was forced to leave school. While she was convalescing at home, her grandfather, who was a tombstone carver, began to nurture her artistic abilities by drawing with her as he sat on her bed. Shortly thereafter, both her grandfather and her mother passed away. Odjig and her sister Winnie were pulled from their home and thrust into a society marked by racism. Like many young people of her time and culture, she was told and began to believe that there was something wrong with being "Indian." Odjig quickly learned not to tell people who she was or where she was from. She explains:

> I left the reserve to find work, to make a living, but all I felt qualified for was housework. I'll never forget my first interview. I was shaking as I knocked on the door. The door opened and the lady seemed to be looking right through me. "I'm here cause I saw your ad wanting a girl to do housework," I stammered. The woman invited me in and told me to sit down. I sat. "You're Indian aren't you?" she said. "Yes," I replied. She stood up. It was obvious the interview was over. I was determined never to be an Indian again. For the next two decades of my life I lived a successful lie. I found becoming a non-Indian not beyond my reach. People often asked if I was Spanish, French, Italian, etc., and my answer was always "Yes" and I did get jobs.[4]

As time passed, Odjig would come not only to symbolize her own culture but to represent Canada's identity. She and her sister moved to Toronto to escape the racism they had experienced. During the war years, she worked in factories making guns and canning dog food. Then, she explains, "My sister and I went to a restaurant and asked if they would give us credit until we got paid. They did."

It was at a dance in Toronto that Odjig met her first husband, Paul Somerville, who was part Mohawk. Paul became the father of her only child, Stanley, and encouraged his wife's talent. They moved together to British Columbia, but in 1960 an automobile accident left Odjig a widow. She worked at her art to compensate for her pain and loss. In 1963 she married her current husband, Chester Beavon, who had great faith in her dreams and supported her pursuit of them.

As a child, she had wanted to be a teacher and would dragoon other children into her "classroom" in an old chicken coop. As a young woman, she had been tempted to become a flamenco dancer. But then her sister-in-law, Rosemary Fisher, held the first pow-wow on Wikwemikong, the eastern side of Manitoulin Island, and at this point she decided to embrace her Aboriginal identity and to dance pow-wow. Yet her life quest was to be a visual artist. She wanted to create and sell her art works, and she knew that she needed a gallery of her own in which Aboriginal arts could be celebrated.

To understand this need, one must understand the times. Although Aboriginal people of North America were referred to as "Indians," the country's leadership provided some solace. Lester B. Pearson, who was in the Prime Minister's office from 1963 to 1968, liked to maintain a connection to the people who had elected him. In 1964 he flew in a helicopter to the Wikwemikong pow-wow. There, Tom Peltier and Odjig had organized a display of 110 art works by Aboriginal artists. On Pearson's advice, the Ministry of Cultural Affairs purchased the entire display, which included a number of Odjig's works. This became the foundation for the National Collection of Native Art, now called The National Indian Art Collection, which is housed by The Department of Indian and Northern Affairs Canada in The Indian Art Centre in Gatineau, Quebec.

Still, many Canadian galleries had yet to "discover" the contemporary work of Aboriginal artists. The romantic imagery of Aboriginal people promoted on TV and in films portrayed people of the past. This ideological screen limited opportunities for Aboriginal people, as they were not seen in a contemporary context. Art historians were reluctant to discuss Aboriginal art on a serious level, forcing a discourse that focussed on the "legends of a dying race." Art historian Celia Rabinovitch explains:

> Romantic ideology, which dominated European thought since the mid-nineteenth century, purported that indigenous cultures, which were negatively characterized as "primitive," were lower on the evolutionary chain of culture and therefore less evolved, and in contradiction, closer to the origins of human culture, and therefore positive. They were sought after as the "original culture" (*ur-kultur*) created by the imaginings of Germanic/Austrian thought. In German Romantic ideology, the aboriginal culture's exposure to Western culture produced a syncretized culture contaminated by Western European contact, hence further away from the purity of origins so avidly sought by European Romantic thinkers since the mid-nineteenth century.[7]

Beavon and Odjig moved from Easterville to Koostatak, then to Ashen, and finally to Winnipeg. In the 1970s Odjig was invited to exhibit her works in Montreal, the USA, Japan, England and France, before finally exhibiting in Manitoba, where she was living. In 1972 Jacqueline Fry curated *Treaty Numbers 23, 287, 1171: Three Indian Painters of the Prairies*, which was shown at the Winnipeg Art Gallery from August 12 to October 10 of that year. The three painters were Jackson Beardy, Alex Janvier, and Daphne Odjig Beavon. This was a groundbreaking exhibition, bringing contemporary Aboriginal art to the forefront for the Canadian public to acknowledge. Yet Odjig wanted to have her work discussed for its own sake, insisting, "My aspiration is to excel as an artist in my own individual right, rather than to be accepted because I am an Indian."[8]

A Learning Curve: Reproductions

During this time Odjig had been creating ink sketches of the Cree of Chemahawin at Easterville in Manitoba, while living there with Beavon who was engaged in development work. These sketches attracted praise from co-workers of her husband. This approval and recognition encouraged Odjig and her husband to create cards from her work and to offer them to the general public. When they moved to Winnipeg in 1970, both Odjig and Beavon decided to commit themselves full time to Aboriginal art, and so they founded Odjig Indian Prints of Canada Limited, which produced a catalogue to market reproductions of Aboriginal art across the country.

Odjig Indian Prints of Canada sold unnumbered, unsigned serigraphs, children's books, hasty notes, and Christmas cards. The serigraphs sold for four to twenty dollars and included works by Norval Morrisseau, Jackson Beardy, Carl Ray, Moses Bignell, Eddie Cobiness, and Robert Bruce James. The hasty notes were reproductions of her sketches of the Cree at Chemahawin. One dollar and twenty-five cents bought a pack of ten. One could purchase twelve Indian legend notes in a burlap folder for the sum of three dollars and fifty cents.

Unfortunately Odjig and her husband had no knowledge of printmaking processes. Odjig had received no formal training in the medium and the people encouraging her did not have a background in the arts. Like the general public, they did not understand that different techniques of printmaking are valued differently for their "authenticity" in the art world. A reproduction is the action or process of simply making a copy of something, for example, through photography. Lithography is the process of printing from a flat surface treated so as to repel the ink except where it is required for printing. A serigraph is a design printed by means of a silk screen. And an etching requires engraving metal, glass, or stone by coating it with a protective layer, drawing on it with a needle, covering it with acid to attack the parts the needle has exposed, and using it to produce prints.

Odjig and her husband soon came to understand the difference in types of artist's prints. Formally trained artists told her she had ruined her career by producing reproductions. She wanted to do it just the same in order to document the lives of the people of the North. Friends told her it was better to have made these reproductions than calendar art. It seemed everyone had an opinion on how an artist should create and promote his or her work. As she explains, "They told me that was the end of my career, but I think it got my name out there."

Odjig's work began to appear in other media. Ginn and Company published ten books with stories and illustrations by Odjig that were included by the Manitoba Department of Education in its curriculum for kindergarten to Grade 4. These books also received notice in the *Winnipeg Tribune* of December 23, 1971, in the article "Artist's books about Nanabush relates tales of Indian legends."

Odjig Indian Prints of Canada also produced Christmas cards designed by children. Their 1973 catalogue explains that "[a] contest was held in the spring of '72 by 'Odjig' Indian Prints, inviting Native children to participate in a children's art competition to design Christmas cards for the revised catalogue. Designs were selected, and the children awarded prizes. Grade 1 students from South Indian Lake, Manitoba captured all prizes in the Canada -wide contest."

At the same time, Odjig's work in the collection of Indian Affairs was being exhibited across Canada. Dr. Herbert Schwarz was one of the people who saw her work and was impressed. In 1973 he hired her to illustrate his book *Tales from the Smokehouse*,[12] a series of erotic stories collected from Aboriginal sources. Odjig remembers, "I would send him a drawing and he would send it back telling me to make the genitals bigger and bigger. I was scared they would start to look like a horse."[13]

She did make them bigger, until Schwarz was satisfied.

Schwarz was a friend of Jacqueline Picasso, the wife of Spanish artist Pablo Picasso, whom Odjig admired. Schwarz presented Jacqueline with a work of Odjig's, and eventually Picasso himself came to see Odjig's work and speak of it very favourably. Picasso asked Odjig if she would like to receive one of his works; however, she saw no reason to add his work to her collection. Jacqueline's suicide later ended Odjig's connection with Picasso.

A Gallery of Distinction

Alongside their print company, Odjig and Beavon opened a craft and gift shop, which soon changed into a gallery for Aboriginal artists looking for a place to promote their art. Many artists would at first drop in to try and sell their artwork, and Odjig often bought it. They came back to have a place where they could discuss their work with an educated viewer, to plan their career, or just for a visit. Odjig says, "Those were exciting days, and you had support from people."[14]

Inspired by their success with the print company and by the support of many Aboriginal artists, Odjig and Beavon opened the Warehouse Gallery at 331 Donald Street in Winnipeg on November 30, 1974.[15] Their opening exhibition featured drawings, water-colours, acrylic and oil works, as well as Odjig's limited edition prints produced for *Tales from the Smokehouse*. The official opening took place a week later on December 8, 1974.[16] Since mainstream galleries were not involving themselves with Aboriginal art, Odjig felt she had to make a change. Both she and Beavon worked hard to establish the gallery as a place for Aboriginal art, regardless of form or media. Odjig and Beavon brought both Native and non-Native communities together in their promotion of Aboriginal art. For them it was never an "either/or" situation; both communities were welcome in the spirit of the arts.

A few people of vision recognized the phenomenon taking place in Manitoba. One of them was Jacqueline Fry of the Winnipeg Art Gallery, who had curated *Treaty Numbers 23, 287, 1171* and mounted other exhibitions of Aboriginal art. Another was Bernard Polly, Head of the Art Department at the University of Brandon, Manitoba, who promoted the work of Odjig and Carl Ray in Brandon. Polly showed Odjig how to scale a painting so that she could paint the mural at Peguis High School in Hodgson, Manitoba.

Odjig's Brandon exhibition drew a lot of attention. *The Brandon Sun* reported:

> Daphne Odjig (O-jig) together with her husband Chester Beavon, a Welshman and community development officer at Koostatak, Manitoba, lent the Brandon University campus event a special fillip. Prof. Bruce MacFarlane discovered Daphne Odjig's work at a Banff School of Fine Arts seminar, where samplings of her acrylics formed a display. [...] The 78 paintings and pen-and-inks emblazon the walls of [the] music building foyer and the lower-floor lounge of the Education building. [...] When the Brandon exhibition of the Odjig show comes down on Nov. 24, it moves immediately to the Viscount Gort Motor Hotel for a four-day showing in Winnipeg.[17]

When Odjig talks of her success she notes all the people who helped her. The Manitoba Indian Brotherhood gave her artistic career promotional support and welcomed the opportunity to celebrate Aboriginal arts. Isaac Beaulieu, who was secretary-treasurer of the Indian Brotherhood at the time of Odjig's Brandon exhibition, said, "The brotherhood approves of any demonstration of special Indian arts and skills."[18] The Indian Brotherhood also sponsored the exhibition at Viscount Gort Motor Hotel. They supported the artists in trying to portray their culture as contemporary, living, and growing.

Odjig's goal in life has been to keep the stories and beliefs alive and circulating for people to come, and to inspire other artists to exhibit their culture-based works. She explains that this is necessary because "[m]any of our traditions are disappearing from the Canadian scene. Even dog sleds are being replaced by ski mobiles. If you destroy our traditions you also destroy our soul."[19]

In the past, people had been put in prison for celebrating their culture. Children had been taken away from their families so that they would not hear the kinds of stories Odjig was telling. She wanted the people to know it was safe to talk about these things again.

The Indian Group of Seven

Many names have been used to describe this prodigious group of artists: the "Second Group of Seven," the "Indian Group of Seven," or "Indian Art by the Seven."[20] All of these names were used to identify the group of people who in November 1973 founded the Professional Native Artists Incorporation. The press loved the name, as it exposed a cultural duality in the art world that continues to this day. This group would never have come together if not for Odjig, who recruited the members one by one. The union encouraged and inspired them to carry on in their individual careers.

Odjig first met Jackson Beardy, who was friends with Carl Ray and Norval Morrisseau. She then met Ray at one of his exhibitions. Eventually she encountered Morrisseau, who had been exhibiting his work successfully since 1962. After speaking with Odjig, Alex Janvier decided to travel to Winnipeg to meet the group. Joseph Sanchez met her in 1971, when he wandered into the gallery. The final member of the group was Eddie Cobiness.

Jackson Beardy was Cree, born in 1944 at Garden Hill Reserve, Manitoba. He attended Portage Indian School, a residential school in Portage la Prairie. This experience was to haunt him throughout his life, creating difficulties in deciding where he belonged in the world. Jackson died at the age of forty in Winnipeg.

Eddie Cobiness was Anishnabe, born in 1933 in the Canada-U.S. border town of Warroad, Minnesota. He soon moved to Buffalo Point Reserve in Manitoba. He was self-taught and worked in oil, acrylic, water-colour, pen and ink, and coloured pencil. He signed his later works with his treaty number, 47. This style of signing protested the Federal Government's policy of denying Aboriginal people their identities. He died in 1996.

Alex Janvier is Dene, born in 1935 and raised on the Le Goffe Reserve in Cold Lake, Alberta. His formal studies began in 1956 at the Southern Alberta Institute of Technology and Art in Calgary. He graduated in 1960 with a diploma in Fine Arts. His works are filled with political and social commentaries and are recognizable by a free-flowing design influenced by beadwork. From 1966 to 1977, Alex signed his work with his treaty number, 287.

Norval Morrisseau is Anishnabe, born in 1931 at Sandy Point Reserve, Ontario. Named Copper Thunderbird, he is known as the Father of the Woodland Art Movement. Raised by his grandparents, Morrisseau was close to his grandfather, who was a shaman. At one point Morrisseau broke with the community over the use of Midewiwin scroll imagery in his works. In 1986, he was appointed Grand Shaman of the Ojibwa.

Carl Ray was Cree, born in 1942 at Sandy Lake Reserve, Ontario. His name was Tall Straight Poplar. He was editor and publisher of Kitawin News and compiled a book, *Sacred Legends of the Sandy Lake Cree*. Ray was a self-taught painter and printmaker. He assisted Morrisseau on his mural commission for the Indians of Canada Pavilion at Expo '67 in Montreal. He also worked as a workshop teacher at Manitoulin Arts Foundation. His family included medicine people and he illustrated Cree beliefs. He became known for his "x-ray" style of painting, which revealed inner organs and energy lines. Ray was fatally stabbed in 1978 at 35 years of age.

Joseph Sanchez and his wife of the time, Anne, moved to Vancouver from Arizona during the Vietnam War period. Sanchez had always wanted to live in Montreal, so they headed east and got far as Saint Anne, Manitoba. It was the closest they ever came to Montreal.

He recounts:

> In 1971 I had the good fortune to walk into Odjig Fine Arts in Winnipeg and to meet Daphne Odjig. She encouraged my work with exhibits in her gallery and allowed me to work with her in her studio. It was through Daphne that I met Norval Morriseau, Eddie Cobiness, Jackson Beardy, Carl Ray and Alex Janvier. The result was the formation of Professional Native Artists, Inc., friendships, ideas and a series of exhibitions coast to coast in Canada.[21]

In 2002 Sanchez joined the staff of the Institute of American Indian Arts Museum in Santa Fe, New Mexico as the Curator of Exhibits, where he is now Co-Interim Director.

The male members of the "Indian" Group of Seven did not just want their own careers to blossom through their collaboration. Like Odjig, they wanted to establish sources of funding that would support other artists, inspire the younger generations and bring communities from across Canada together to celebrate being "Indian." These were very high ideals at a time when Aboriginal people had only recently received voting rights and were fighting politically for their human rights.

The Print Years

Many of the works in *Four Decades of Prints* are the original artist's proofs. Throughout the 1970s, Odjig worked with different print shops across the country, including Great Grassland Graphics, Grand Western Canadian Screen Shop, Canadian Native Prints Limited, and Open Studio in Toronto. The Grand Western Canadian Screen Shop opened in 1968 and was run by Bill Lobchuk, and the printer who worked with Odjig there was Ted Howorth. Because of their previous collaboration, Howarth was later contacted by Phillip Gevik of the Gevik Galleries in Toronto to work with Odjig on the print *Picking Flowers* (1981) for the Sick Children's Hospital.

Odjig and Beavon sold the Warehouse Gallery in 1976, and the new owners changed the name to the Wah-Sa Gallery, which meant, in a roundabout way, the "Far Out" Gallery. Along with the Gevik Galleries, the Wah-Sa Gallery also produced works for sale by Odjig. She continued to have exhibitions at the Wah-Sa Gallery for many years. Canadian Native Prints Limited was based in Vancouver, British Columbia. According to Odjig, the owners were originally from Germany and were expert printers. They eventually left Canada to retire to the Cayman Islands.

Odjig feels that her first real print was *Rolling Head*, a serigraph done in 1971, which is now in the collection of the Kamloops Art Gallery. The narrative portrayed in this image retells the infidelity of a woman who had married a chief and had two sons by him. When the chief was away the wife took a lover. Her sons saw what was happening and told their father, who in retaliation cut off her head. The head started to roll after the boys to take revenge on them for telling their father of the unfaithfulness. The boys ran to the river, where the cranes took pity on them and made a bridge with their necks. The boys made their escape to the other side. When the rolling head tried to cross by way of the cranes' necks, they uncrossed them and the rolling head fell into the water and drowned.

Many of Odjig's prints, such as *Nanabush and the Dancing Ducks* (1971) and *Medicine Dream* (1974), depict stories and beliefs from Odjig's culture. Each story expresses a belief and functions as a way to pass on ethics and morals to the next generation. Odjig also produced many works that are intended to pass on the emotions and behaviour important to her community, such as her 1979 prints *Comforting* and *Caring* (from the *Motherhood Series I*) and *Pride*, as well as her 1980 print *Listening*, from the series *Homage to Grandfather Portfolio — dedicated to Jonas Odjig*.

In 1975 El Al Airlines of Israel invited Odjig to tour the country and record her impressions in art. This trip resulted in the *Jerusalem* series of limited edition silk screens, among many other works. Odjig had an epiphany in Jerusalem, a feeling that she had been there before, perhaps in another lifetime. Her prints from this visit contain vibrant and true colours of blue, yellow, and reds, which make the paper appear whiter, as if the works were bathed in strong sunlight.

In 1982, Odjig decided she wanted to try different print techniques with Joseph Sanchez in Arizona. She and her sister Winnie, who often travelled with her around the world, left Canada for the south-western state. She explains, "In the 1980s Joseph was always asking me to visit him in Arizona and create some prints with different methods."[22] Following Sanchez's advice, they visited with different artists while in Arizona. Odjig later remarked that the methods they saw produced a change in her way of presenting her subject. She states, "They were all experiments, but they turned out so well: monotype."[23]

The works Odjig produced in Arizona are all untitled; they were made on a small etching press, with Sanchez as the printer. Though much more abstract in style than her signature work, the Odjig sensibility is still visible in the works through the artist's bold use of colour.

Odjig's most recent print is *In Tune with the Infinite*, produced in 2004. This work is filled with colour and the organic forms for which Odjig is famous. Each line ties into another as humans tie into the landscape.

All of Odjig's prints, except for the untitled abstract works from Arizona, have the classic Woodland styling. However, Odjig's sensibility is unique even within this school. Her shapes are organic and she uses darker lines to outline the shapes. Odjig has explained, "My style ... has gone through — realism — impressionism — cubism and non-objective by experimentation. I have tried to evolve my own style using native forms, designs, and colours to express a native Indian Art form that I can call my own."[24]

The repeating circles and arches in Odjig's designs are all a reflection of her past. The arches are from the doorway to her grandfather's room. The circles relate to her grandfather's work as a tombstone carver. As she looked at the tombstones her grandfather carved, she noticed the rounding of the edges. The wings of the Thunderbird circle the images, protecting the figures in *Genesis* (1976), *Western Wall* (1976), *The Rhythm of the Drum* (1977), *Reflections* (1977), and *Folk Singer* (1977). Few of the faces in her prints have a mouth, and if they do, it is a small one. Odjig says, "[My] ovals always seem to be a protective thing."[25]

The colours in the early prints are strong yellows, reds, and fluorescent oranges. These works also include cool, rich browns that draw out the other colours. By the early mid-70s, this palette evolves into earthy muted tones in the next series, only to change again with the *Jerusalem* series of 1976, which makes use of the bright colours that Odjig witnessed in that area of the world. The artist's lines become stronger and more defined as each series evolves. In the later works, all of her developed skills come together.

The Indian in Transition, the mural Odjig had been commissioned to paint for the National Museum of Man in Ottawa in 1974, and which was completed in 1978, captured Odjig's hopes for future generations while holding true to the spirit of her Pottawatomi nation. Odjig has collected extensively in her support of emerging artists. She has marched on Parliament Hill for the rights of Native women. She has, throughout her life, consistently looked to the health and well-being of all Native people. Now, in her later years, she rarely speaks in public, preferring to let her work speak for her. In the role of her manager, her son Stanley Somerville now handles all public inquiries and administers her business affairs.

Odjig's only demand has been to be respected as an equal to other Canadian artists. A woman who devoted her life to promoting Aboriginal art in Canada has never had an exhibition at Canada's National Gallery or been the subject of one of their publications. In fact, the National Gallery began collecting her work only after 1999, and has acquired only two paintings.

Today Odjig is open to the future and has no plans, except to enjoy friends and family. If her health allows, she may produce more work, as she is always thinking of creation. However, for the time being she is enjoying the success of all Aboriginal people in what they are accomplishing, stating, "When I get the urge to create, I talk to others and get so excited by their success, it provides me with the nourishment that I need."[26]

The act of creation is from the creator, and Daphne Odjig creates. For her it is a spiritual feeling that not all people may understand. She says, "The deeper you go into the spiritual, very spiritual, you think no one will understand."[27]

Yet looking at her work, we understand.

All our Relations, hi, hi, hi.

Acknowledgements

No one does anything by themselves, and that is true of my writing this essay. First, I would like to thank Daphne Odjig and Chester Beavon for sharing their open hearts and free spirits. Next, I would like to thank Jann Bailey and the staff of the Kamloops Art Gallery for giving me this opportunity. Many people shared their stories: Alex Janvier, Joseph Sanchez, Gary Scherbain from the Wah-Sa Gallery, Phillip Gevik from Gevik Galleries, Ted Howorth and the Manitoulin Expositor. I would like to thank Pat Deadman, Ingrid Jenkner, and Sue Stewart for their support.

Endnotes

1. Daphne Odjig, *To Invent within a Culture*, a lecture presented at the conference *Reflecting Cultures* at the University of Toronto, 1993.

2. Wikwemikong means "Bay of Beavers" in the Anishnabe language (lit.: Wikwet=Bay, Mik=Beaver, Kong="Place of").

3. Manitoulin Island is called Mnidoo Mnis, The Island of the Great Spirit.

4. Daphne Odjig, *To Invent within a Culture*.

5. Daphne Odjig in a telephone interview with the author, February 2005.

6. "Odjig" is the Anishnabe word for the animal known in English as the "fisher."

7. Dr. Celia Rabinovitch, personal correspondence with the author, February 2005.

8. As quoted in Fry, Jacqueline, *Treaty Numbers 23, 287, 1171: Three Indian Painters of the Prairies*, catalogue, (1972, Winnipeg: Winnipeg Art Gallery).

9. Daphne Odjig in a telephone interview with the author, February 2005.

10. "Artist's books about Nanabush relates tales of Indian legends." *Winnipeg Tribune*, December 23, 1971.

11. Odjig Indian Prints of Canada Ltd. catalogue, 1973.

12. *Tales from the Smokehouse* by Herbert T. Schwarz; illustrated by Daphne Odjig. Edmonton: Hurtig, 1974. 102 pages.

13. Daphne Odjg in a telephone interview with the author, March 2005.

14. Daphne Odjig in a telephone interview with the author, April 12, 2005.

15. See the *Winnipeg Free Press*, November 23, 1974, for a preview photo and caption about this opening.

16. Bruce, Barbra, *Le Métis*, December 1974 – January 1975.

17. Rowe, Kaye, "Odjig Show Rates Raves," *The Brandon Sun*, Wednesday, November 13, 1968, p. 15.

18. As quoted in Rowe, K., Op. Cit.

19. Wiseman, Eva, "She paints Indian legends," *The Winnipeg Tribune*, December 25, 1968.

20. See the Wallack Galleries, Ottawa, Ontario, June 1975 invitation.

21. Jospeh Sanchez in a telephone interview with the author, February 2005.

22. Daphne Odjig in a telephone interview with the author, March 2005.

23. Ibid.

24. As quoted in McLuhan, Elizabeth, "Daphne Odjig: Her Art" in E. McLuhan and R.M. Vanderburgh (Eds.) *Daphne Odjig: A Retrospective 1946 – 1985*, (catalogue to the exhibition organized and circulated by the Thunder Bay National Exhibition Centre and Centre for Indian Art, 1985), p. 29.

25. As quoted in Vanderburgh, R.M., "Daphne Odjig: Her Life", in E. McLuhan and R.M. Vanderburgh (Eds.) *Daphne Odjig: A Retrospective 1946 – 1985*, (1985), p. 6.

26. Daphne Odjig in telephone interview with the author, April 2005.

27. Ibid.

Additional Sources

Clifford, James (1988) *The Predicament of Culture*. Cambridge, Massachusetts, and London England: Harvard University Press.

Goldwater, Robert (1938) *Primitivism in Modern Art*. Cambridge, Massachusetts, and London England: The Belknap Press of Harvard University Press.

Hughes, Kenneth James (1979), *Jackson Beardy — Life and Art*. Winnipeg, Manitoba: Canadian Dimension Publishers.

Odjig, Daphne (1998), Address to Wikwemikong's 1998 Graduates. Wikwemikong, Manitoulin Island, July 30.

Podedworny, Carol, and Boyer, Bob (2001) *Odjig: The Art of Daphne Odjig, 1960 – 2000*. Toronto, Ontario: Key Porter Books Limited.

Rabinovitch, Celia (2004) *Surrealism and the Sacred*. Boulder, Colorado: Westview Press.

Robinson, Donald (1997) *Norval Morrisseau*. Toronto, Ontario: Key Porter Books.

Vanderburgh, R.M., and Southcott, M.E. (1992) *A Paintbrush in My Hand*. Toronto, Ontario: Natural Heritage/ Natural History Inc.

Selected Prints from the Exhibition

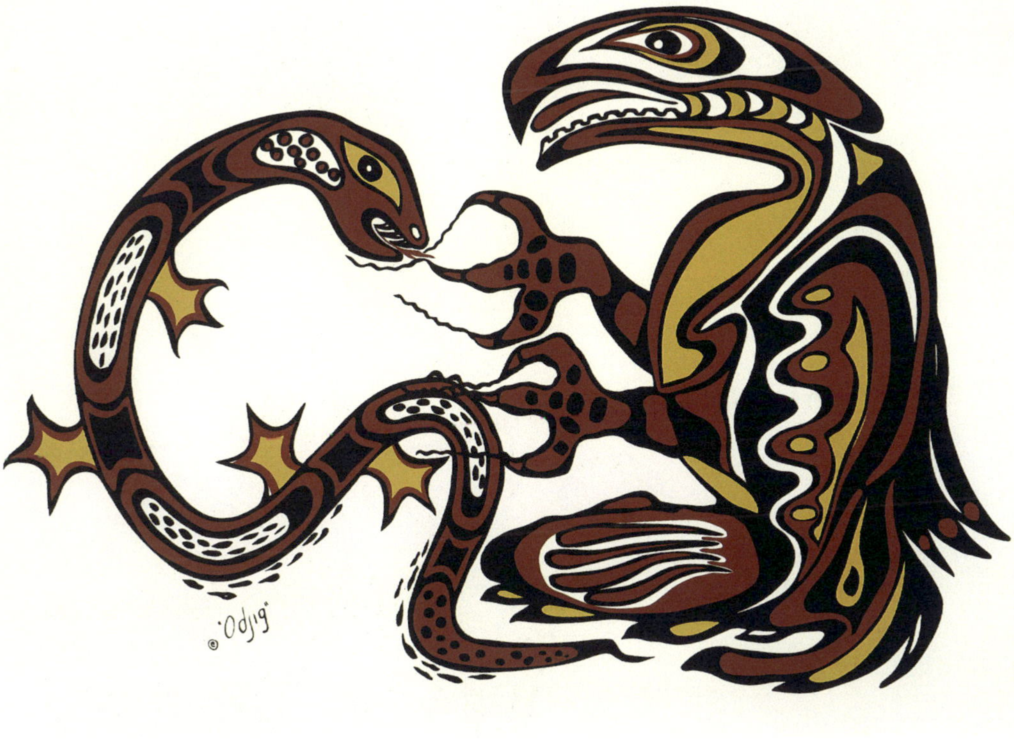

Untitled (The Eternal Conflict), 1968
serigraph on paper, not editioned
34.3 × 51.4 cm
Collection of The Winnipeg Art Gallery
Gift from the Estate of Arnold O. Brigden

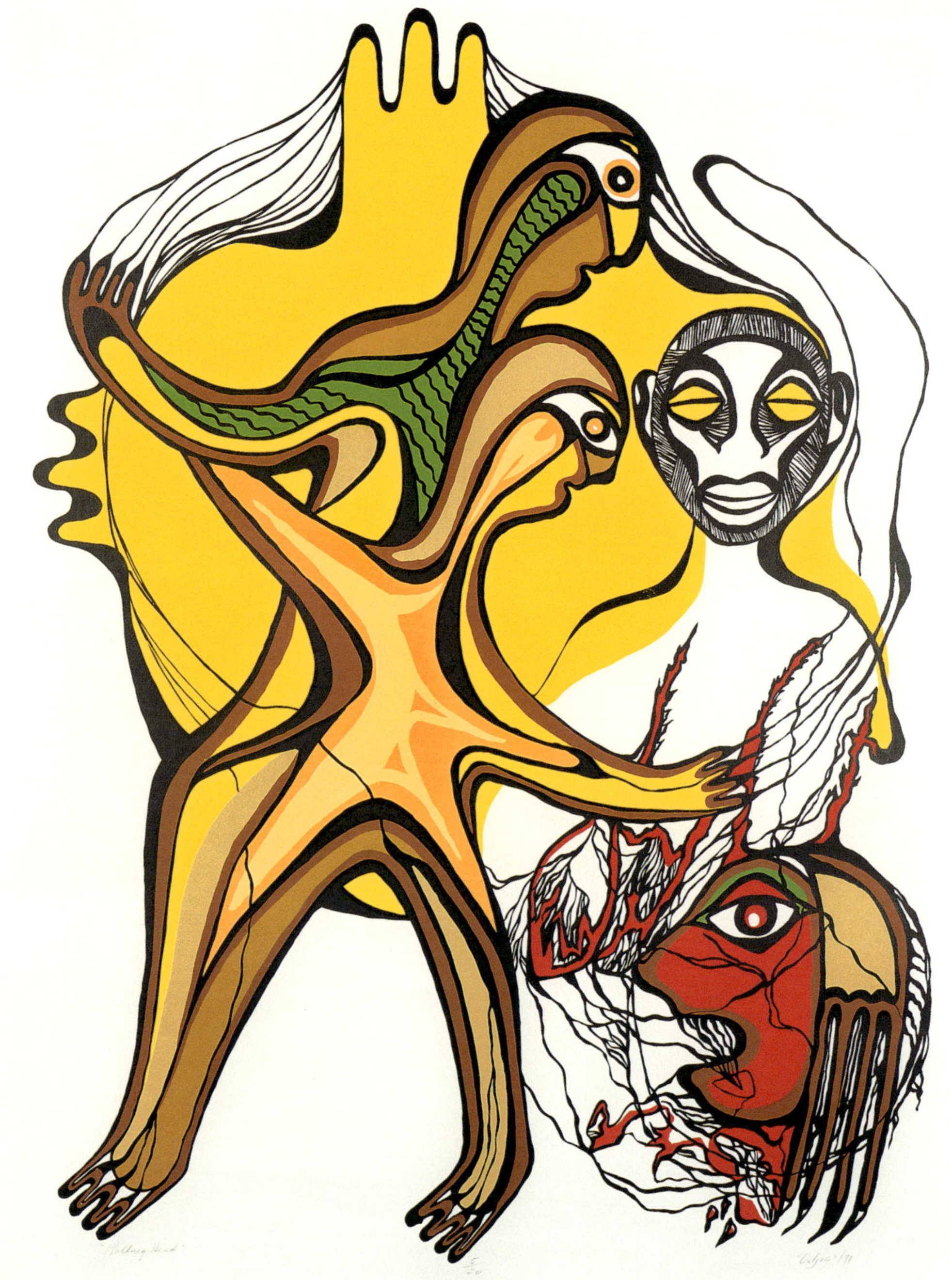

Rolling Head, 1971
serigraph, 5/30
97.5 × 72 cm
Kamloops Art Gallery Collection 2003-073
Gift of Daphne Odjig

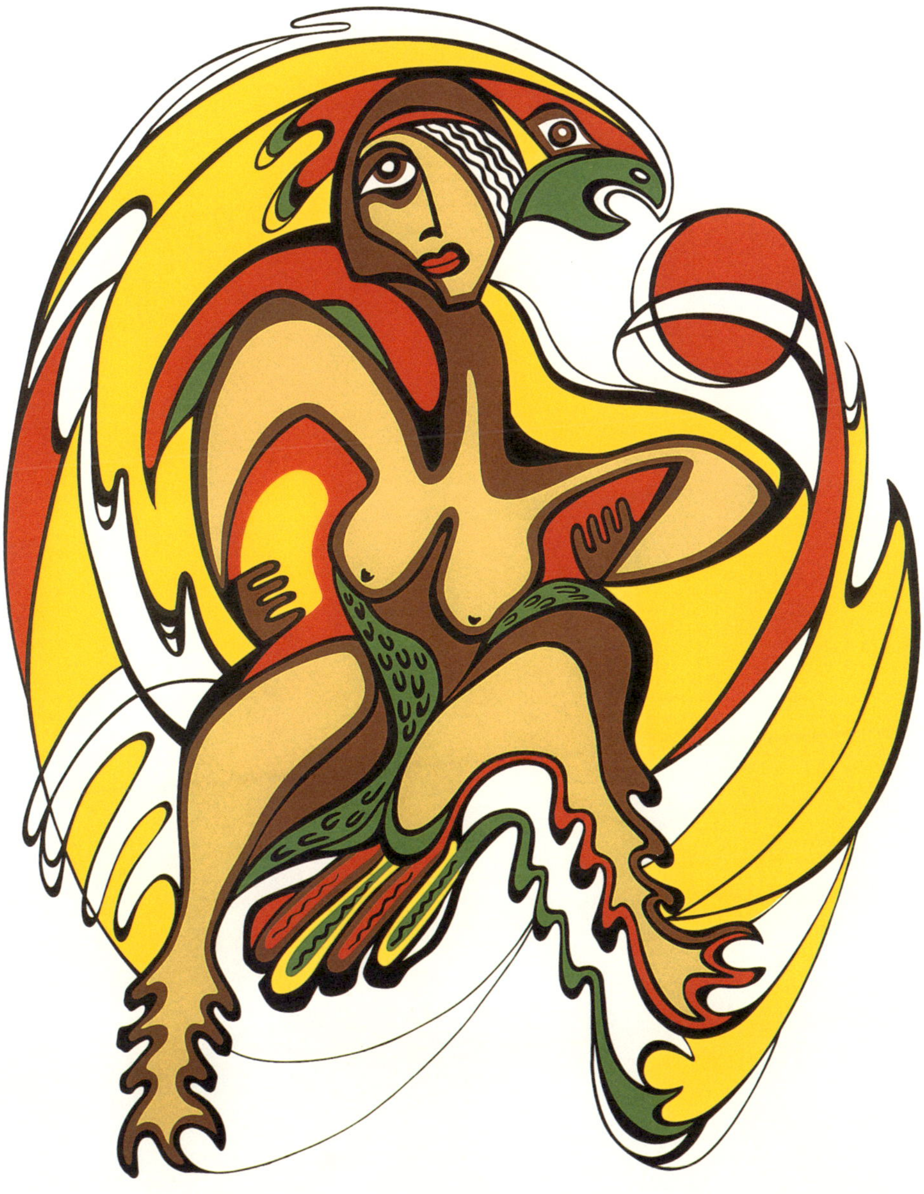

Thunderbird Woman, 1973
serigraph on paper, 13/48
71 × 55.5 cm

Kamloops Art Gallery Collection 2003-041
Purchased with the support of the Canada Council for the Arts Acquisition Assistance program,
Ken Lepin, Elizabeth Illsey, and Linda and Manny Jules

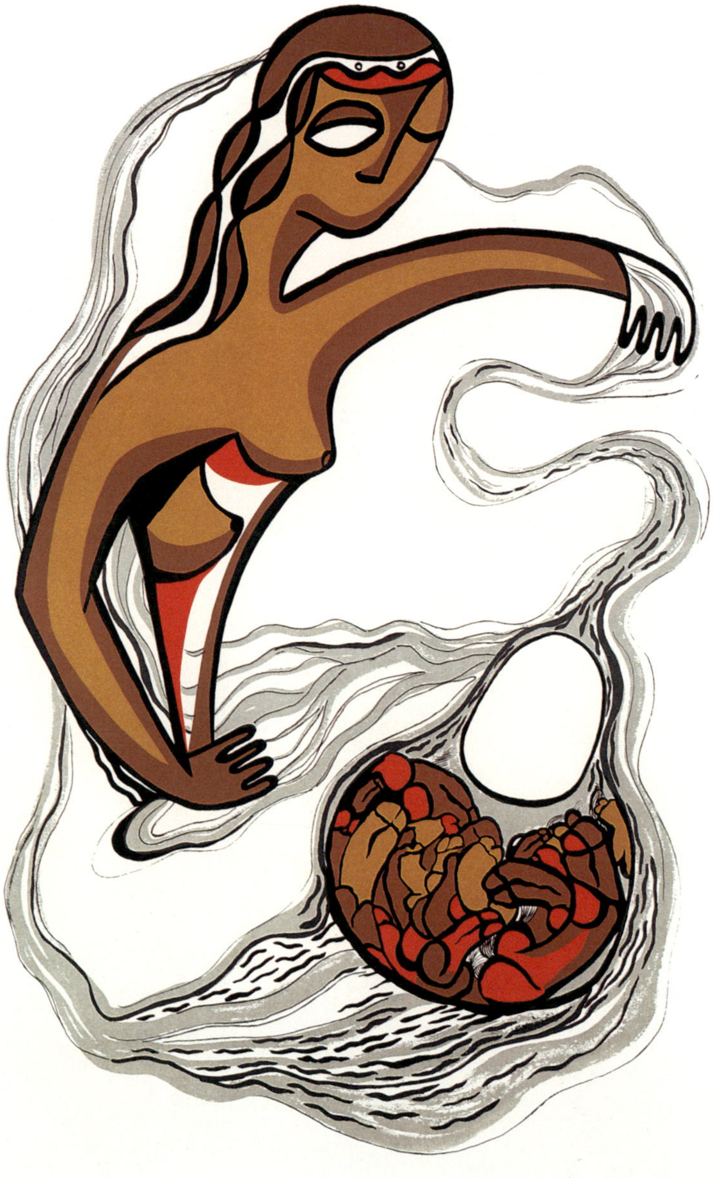

Medicine Dream, 1974
serigraph on paper, 5/60
83 × 53.5 cm
Kamloops Art Gallery Collection 2003-039
Purchased with the support of the Canada Council for the Arts Acquisition Assistance program, Ken Lepin, Elizabeth Illsey, and Linda and Manny Jules

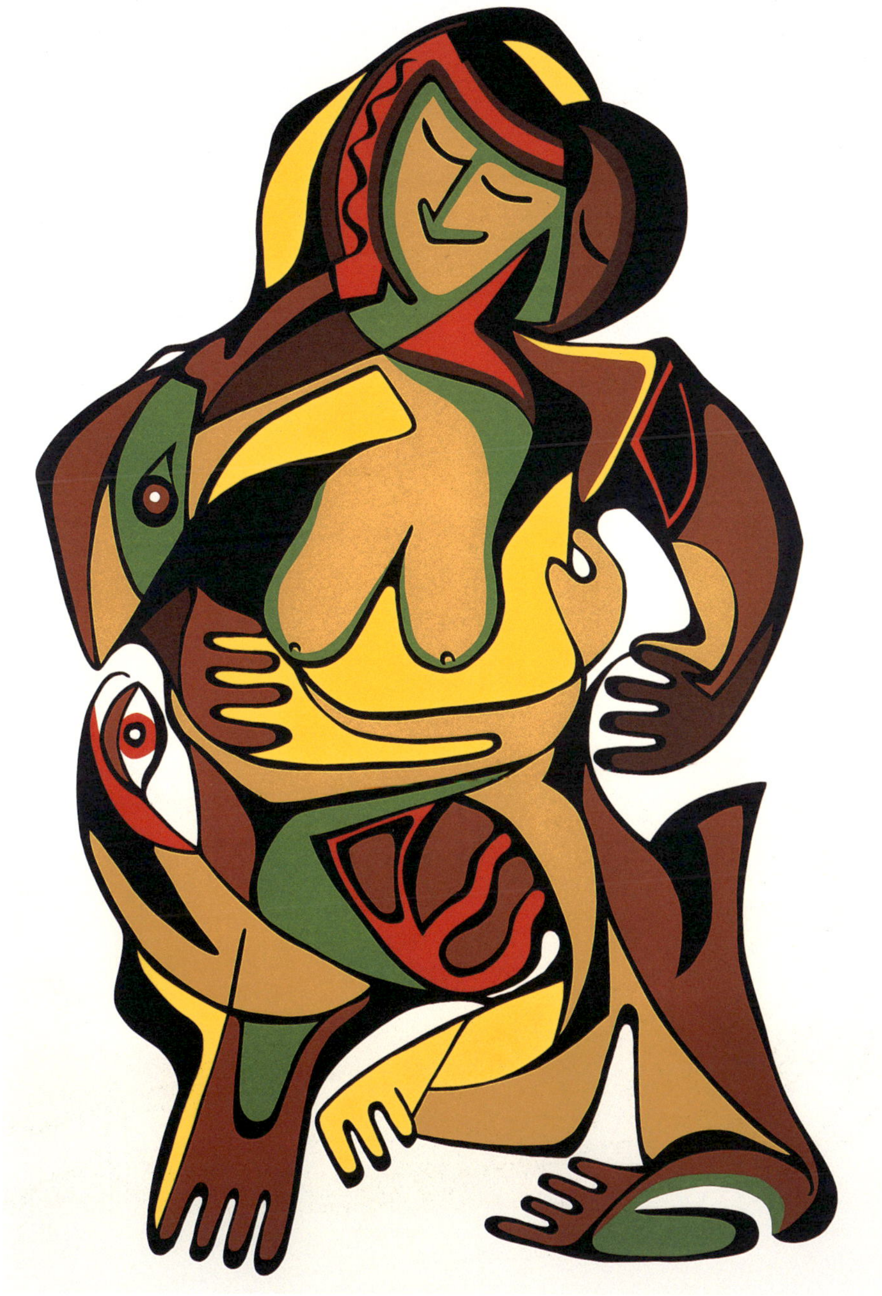

Nanabojou and His Daughter, 1975
serigraph on paper, 11/60
97 × 62 cm

Kamloops Art Gallery Collection 2003-038
Purchased with the support of the Canada Council for the Arts Acquisition Assistance program, Ken Lepin, Elizabeth Illsey, and Linda and Manny Jules

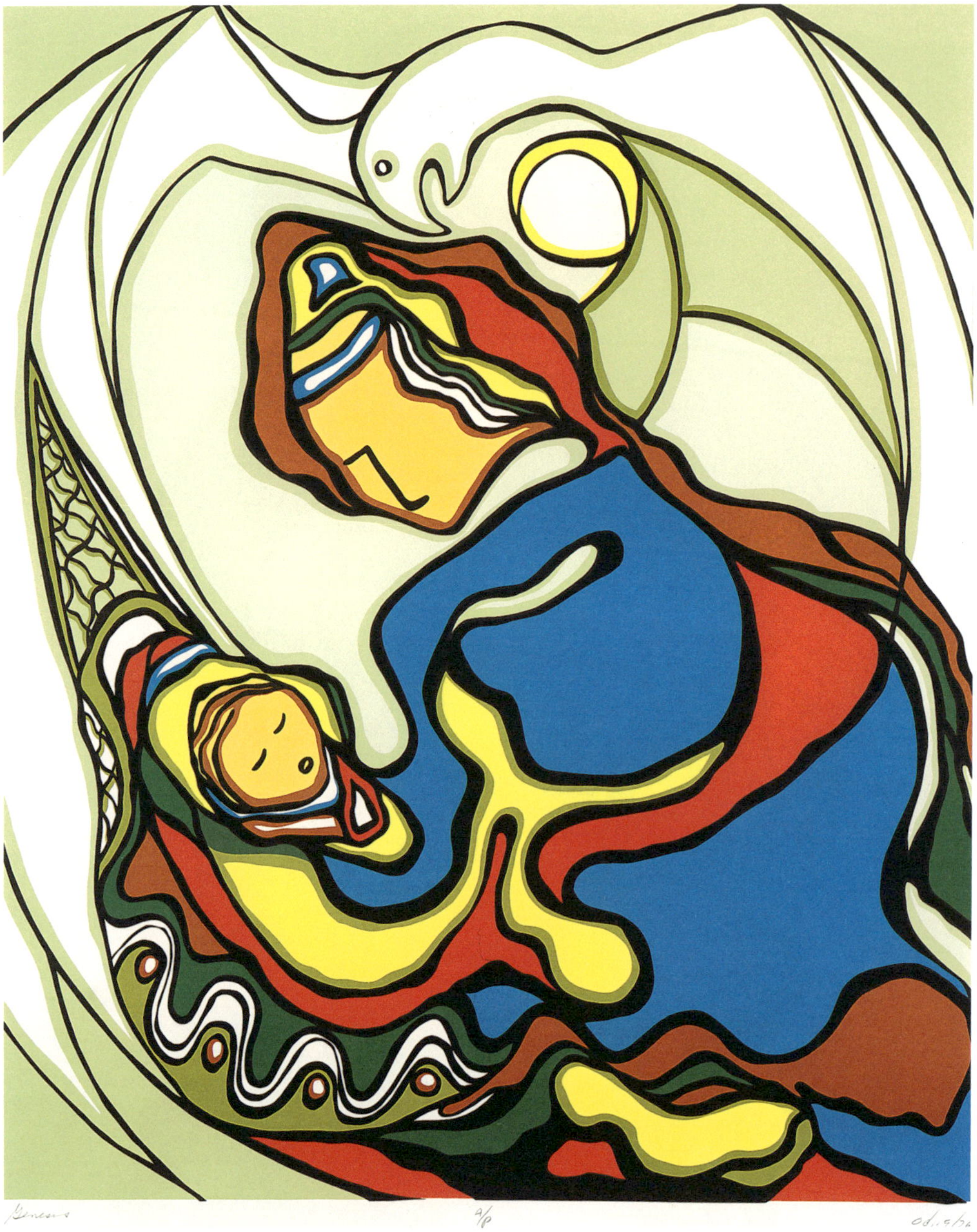

Genesis, 1976
serigraph on paper, AP
73.5 × 61 cm
Collection of Daphne Odjig

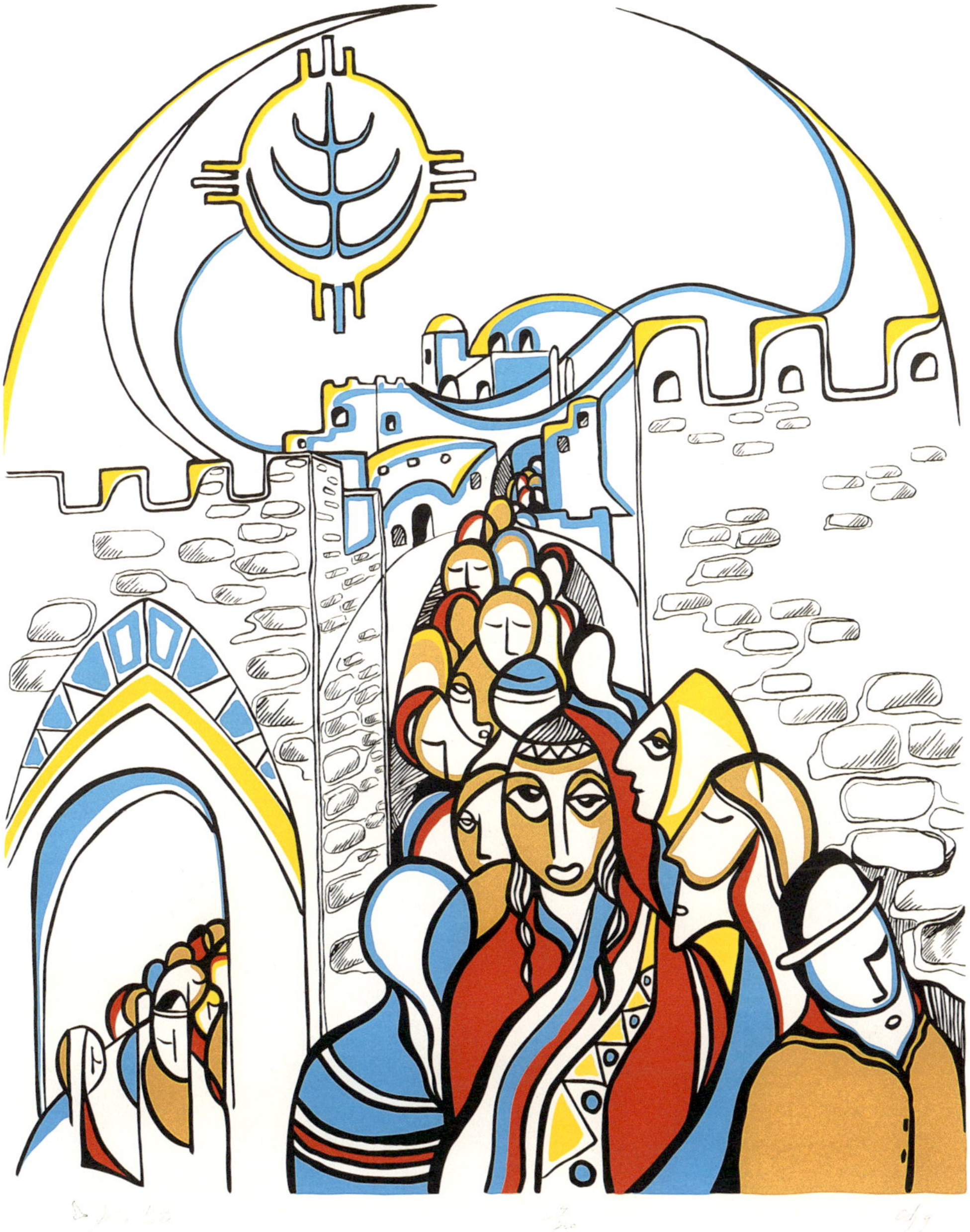

Jaffa Gate, 1976
serigraph on paper, 4/250
63.5 × 50.5 cm
Collection of Stan Somerville

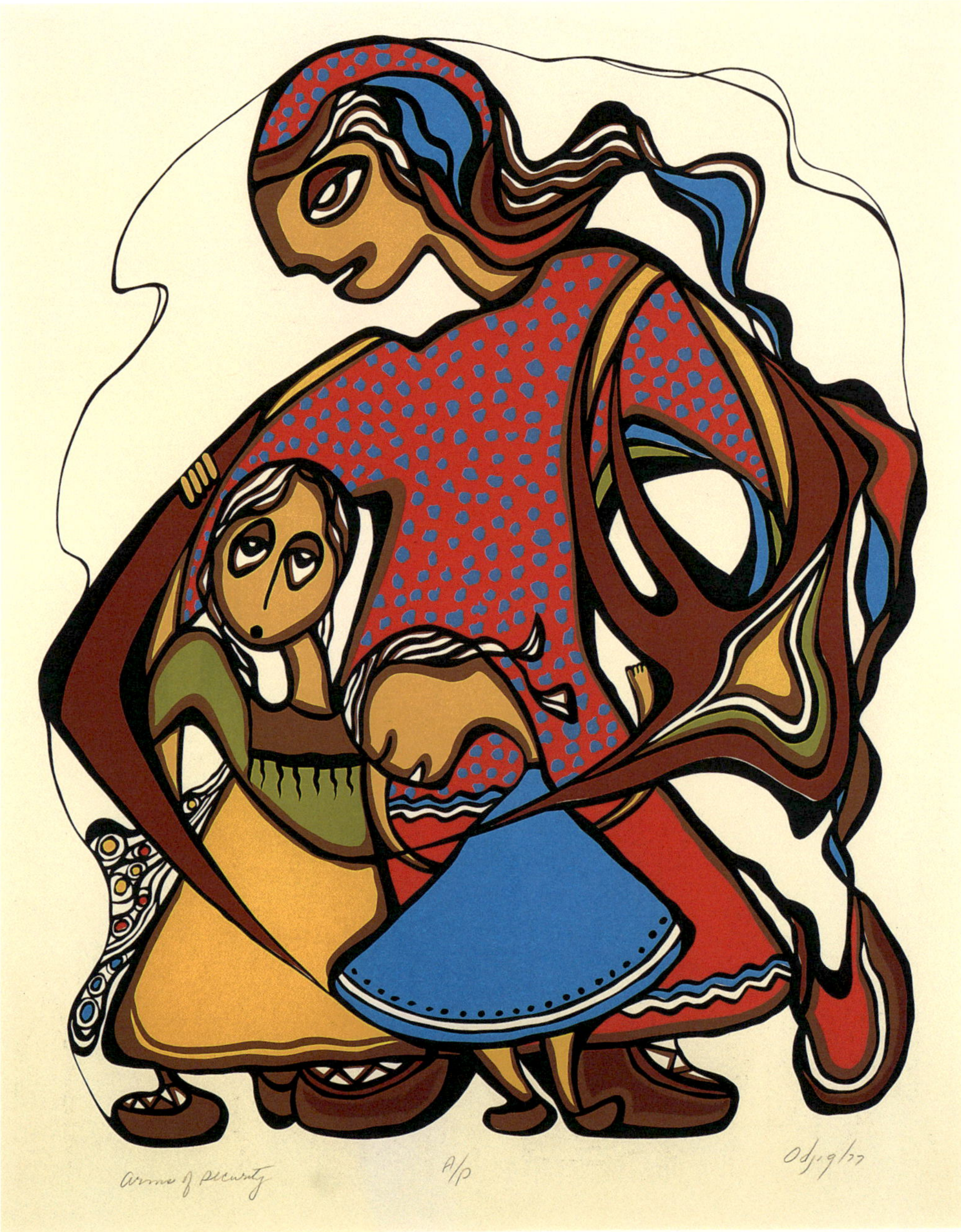

Arms of Security, 1977
serigraph on paper, AP
60.5 × 48 cm
Collection of Stan Somerville

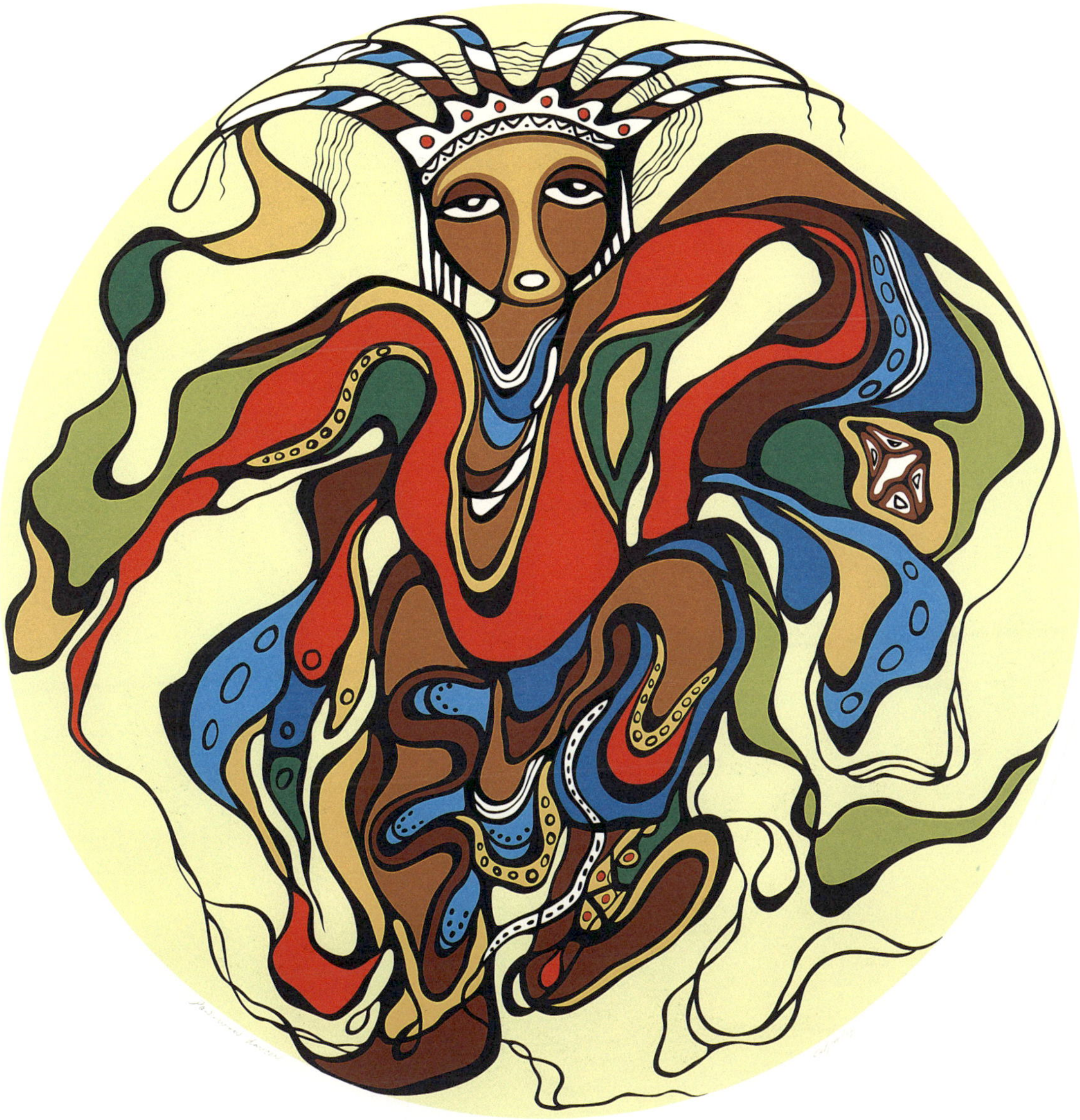

Pow-Wow Dancer, 1978
serigraph on paper, AP
57.3 × 57.3 cm

Kamloops Art Gallery Collection 2003-037
Purchased with the support of the Canada Council for the Arts Acquisition Assistance program, Ken Lepin, Elizabeth Illsey, and Linda and Manny Jules

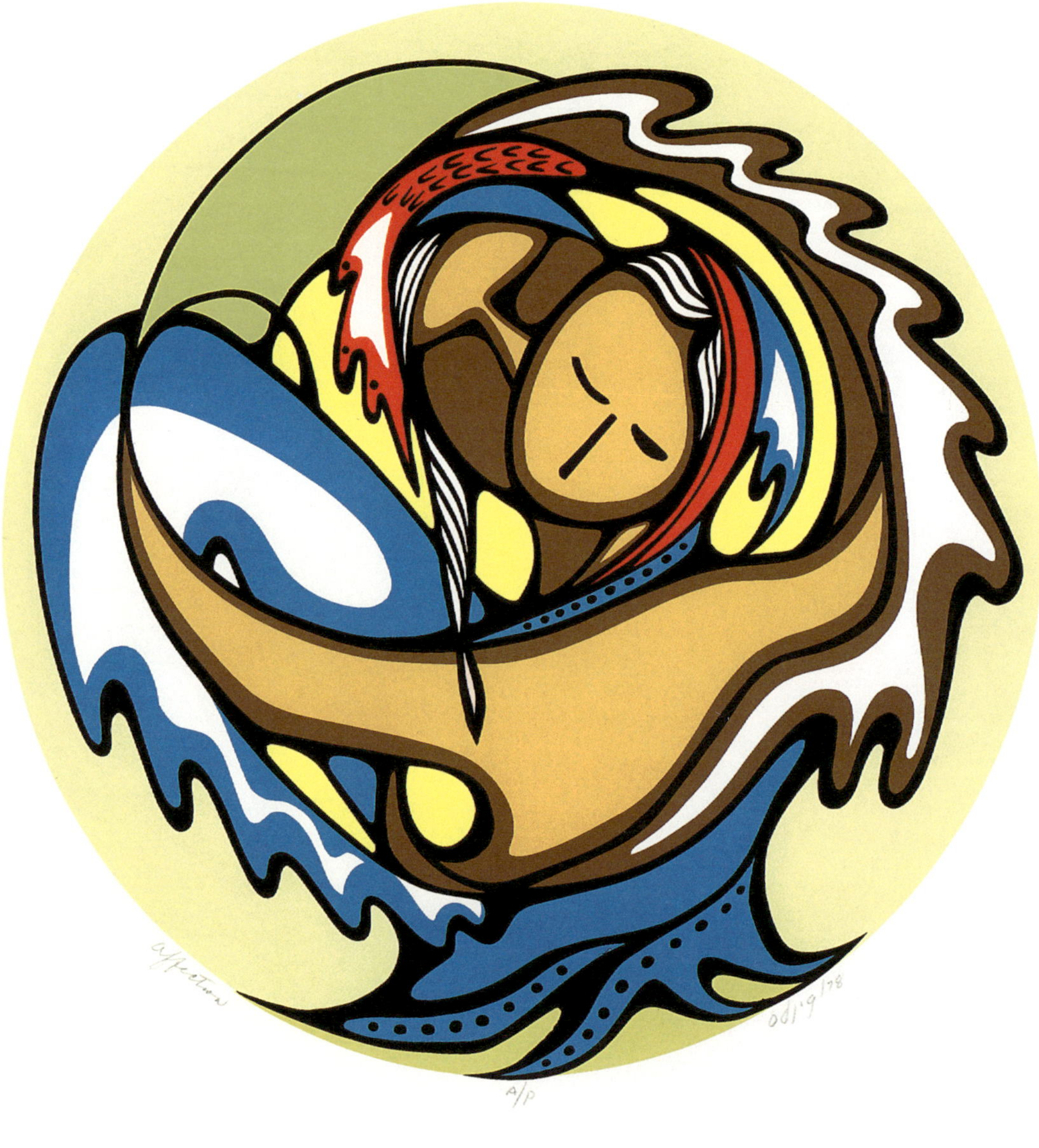

Affection, 1978
serigraph on paper, AP
26.3 × 25.5 cm
Collection of Stan Somerville

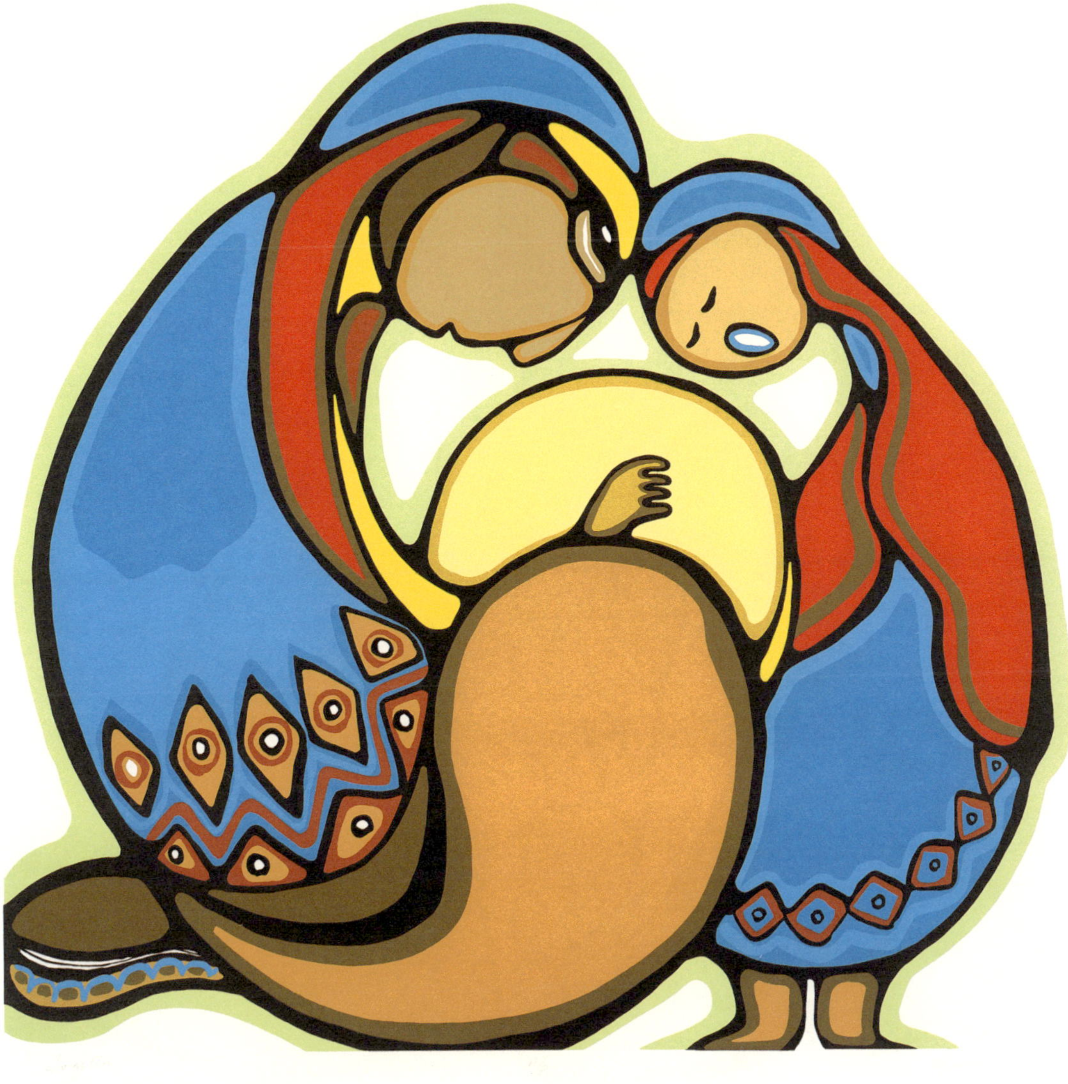

Together, 1979
serigraph on paper, AP
50 × 59.6 cm
Collection of Stan Somerville

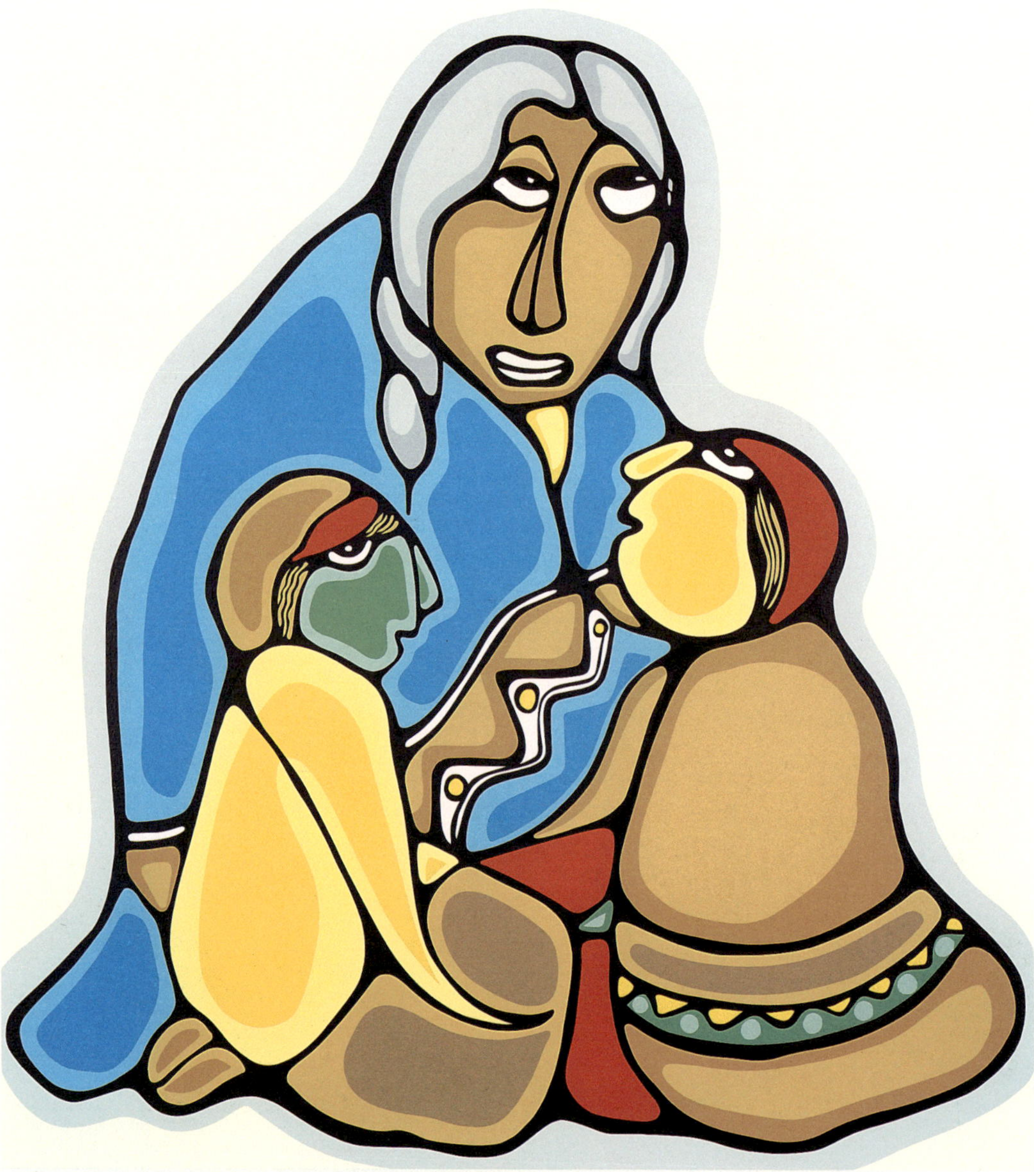

Learning, 1980
serigraph on paper, AP
57 × 50.8 cm
Collection of Stan Somerville

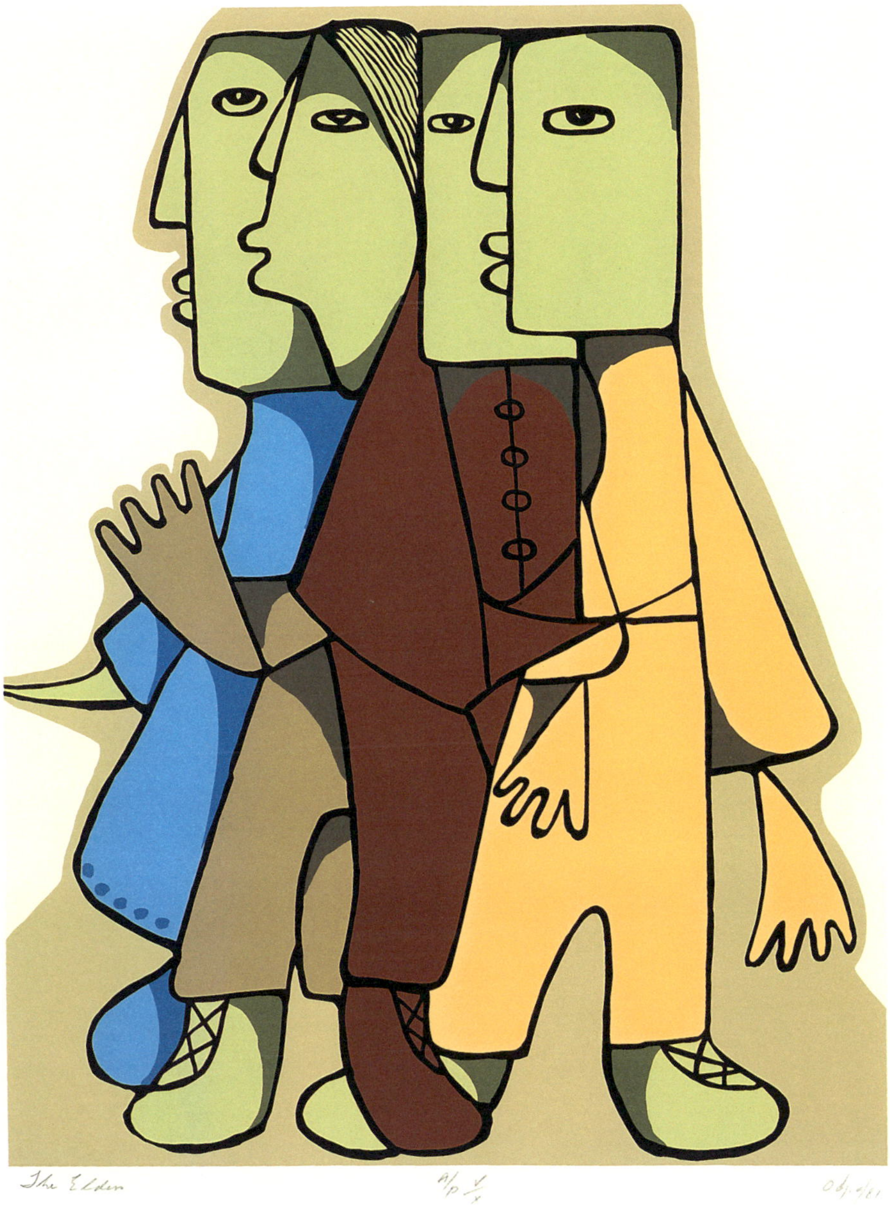

The Elders, 1981
serigraph on paper, AP V/X
35.7 × 28 cm

Kamloops Art Gallery Collection 2003-034
Purchased with the support of the Canada Council for the Arts Acquisition Assistance program,
Ken Lepin, Elizabeth Illsey, and Linda and Manny Jules

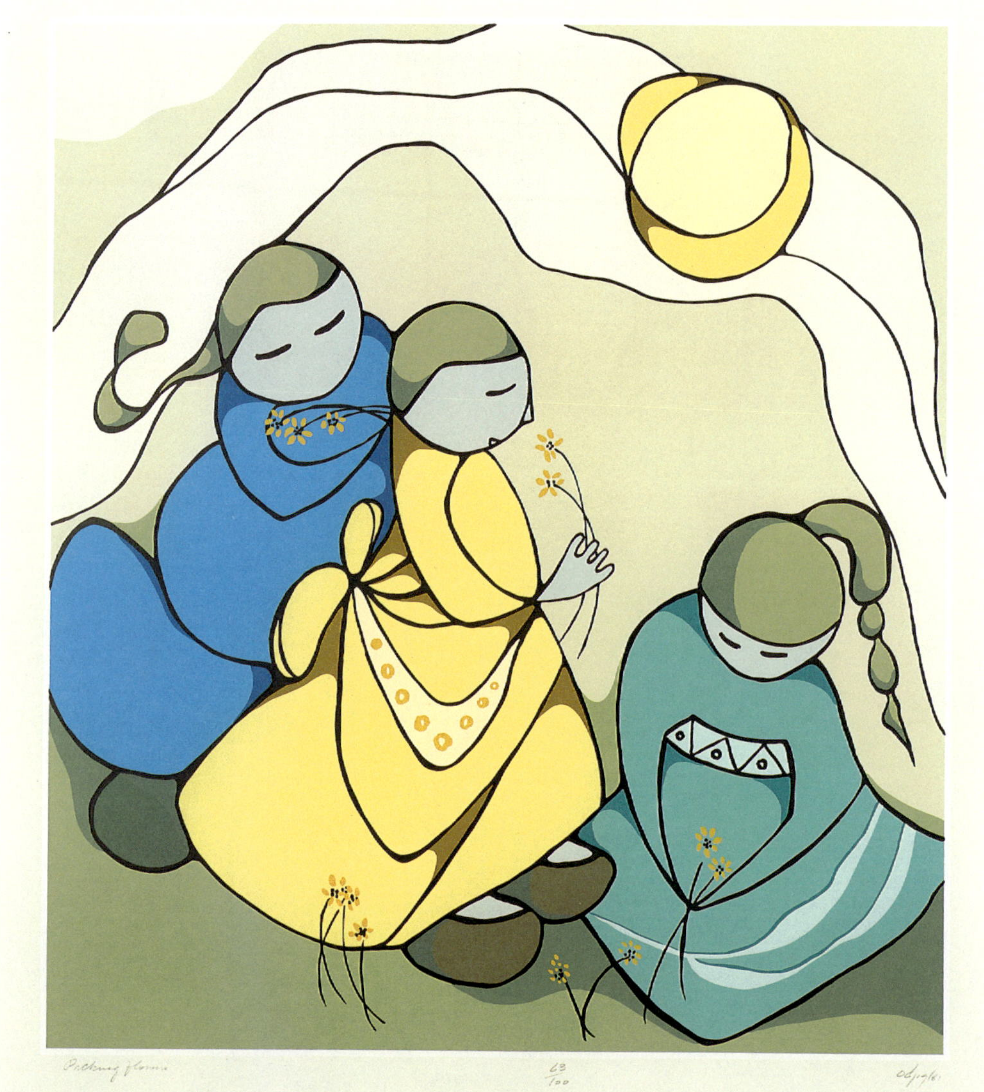

Picking Flowers, 1981
serigraph on paper, 63/100
53.5 × 46.5 cm
Kamloops Art Gallery Collection 2005-008

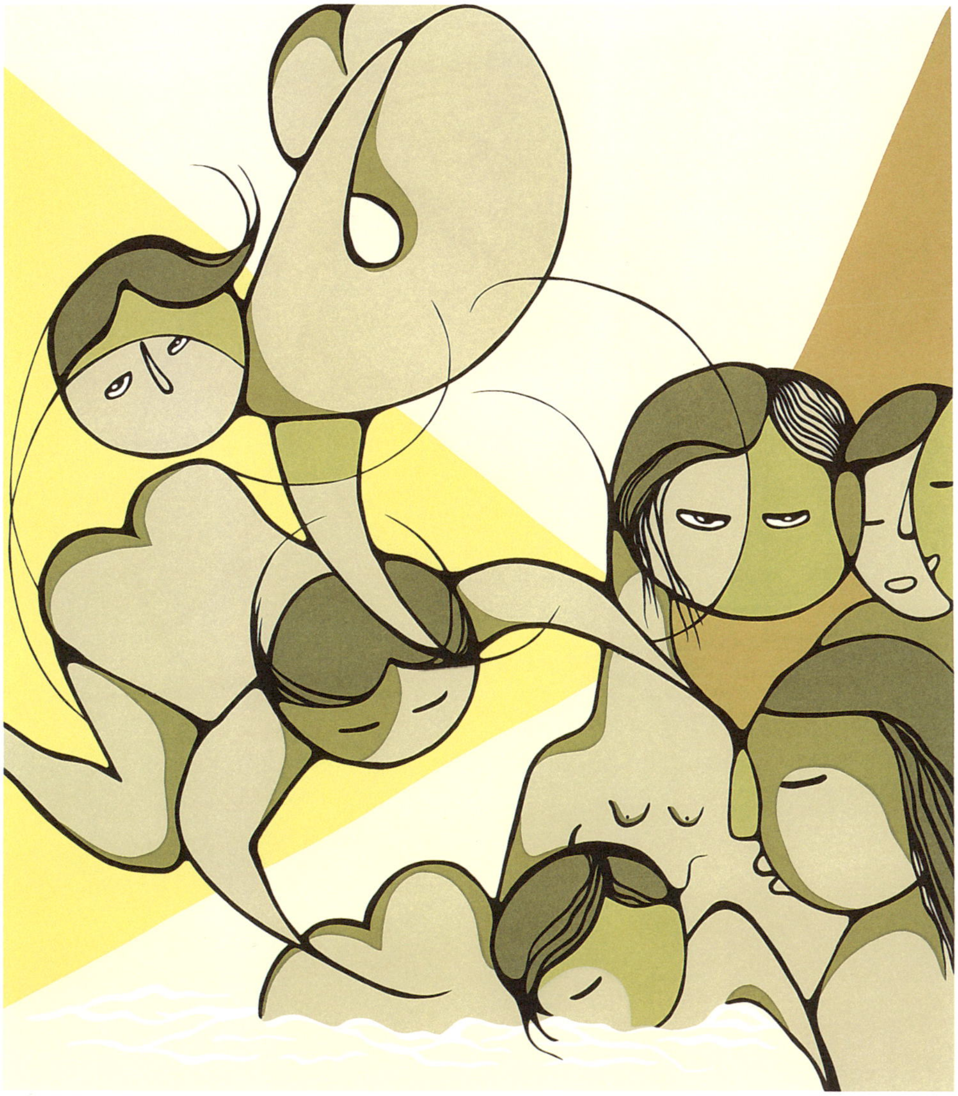

Old Swimming Hole, 1981
serigraph on paper, AP IX/XII
52 × 45.4 cm
Collection of Dave Barron

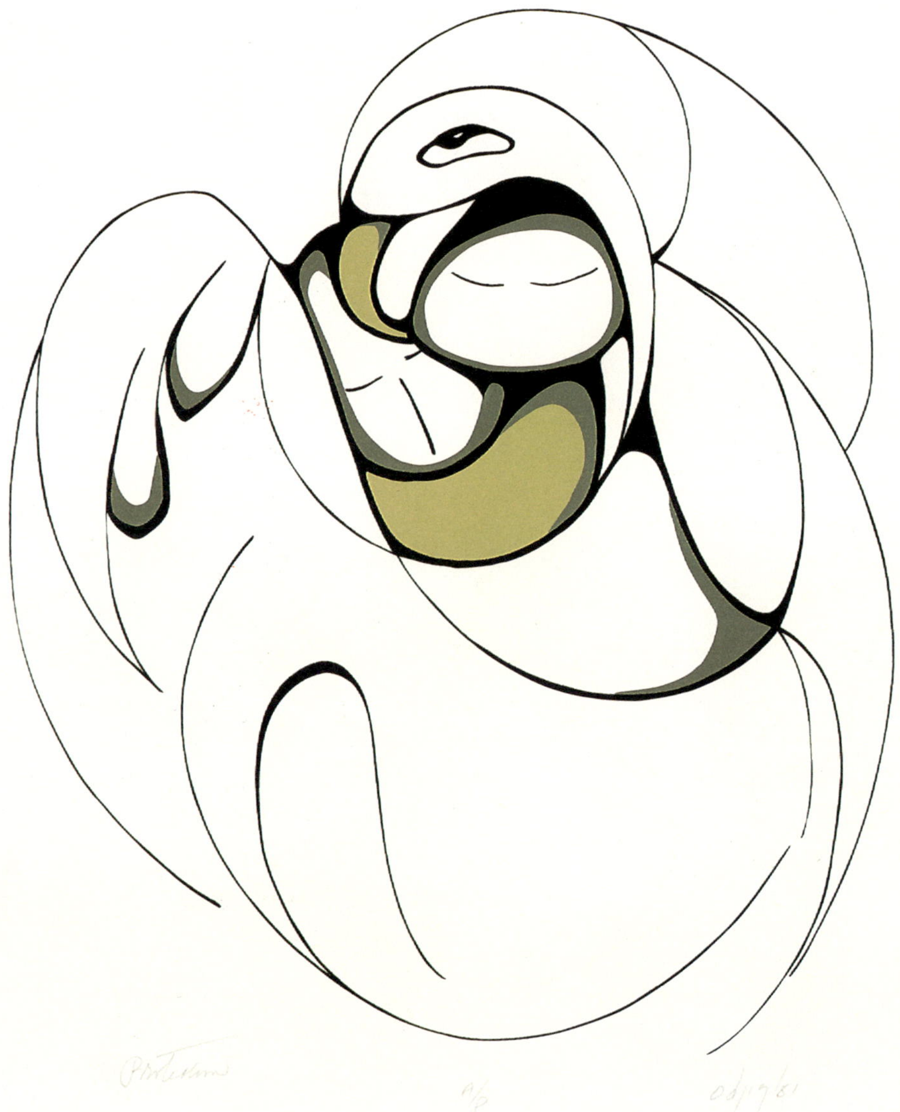

Protection, 1981
serigraph on paper, AP
33.5 × 28 cm
Collection of Stan Somerville

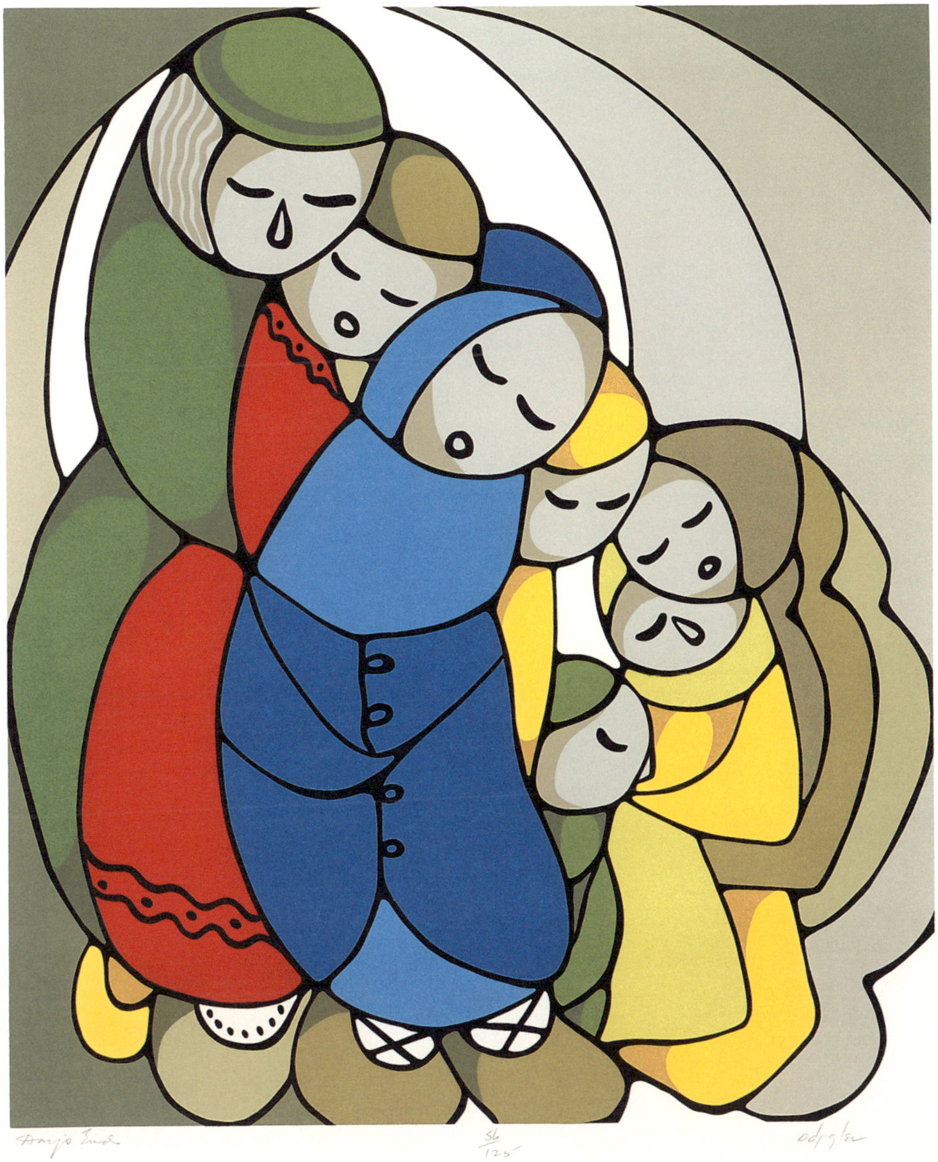

Day's End, 1982
serigraph on paper, 56/125
54.5 × 45.3 cm
Kamloops Art Gallery Collection 2005-001

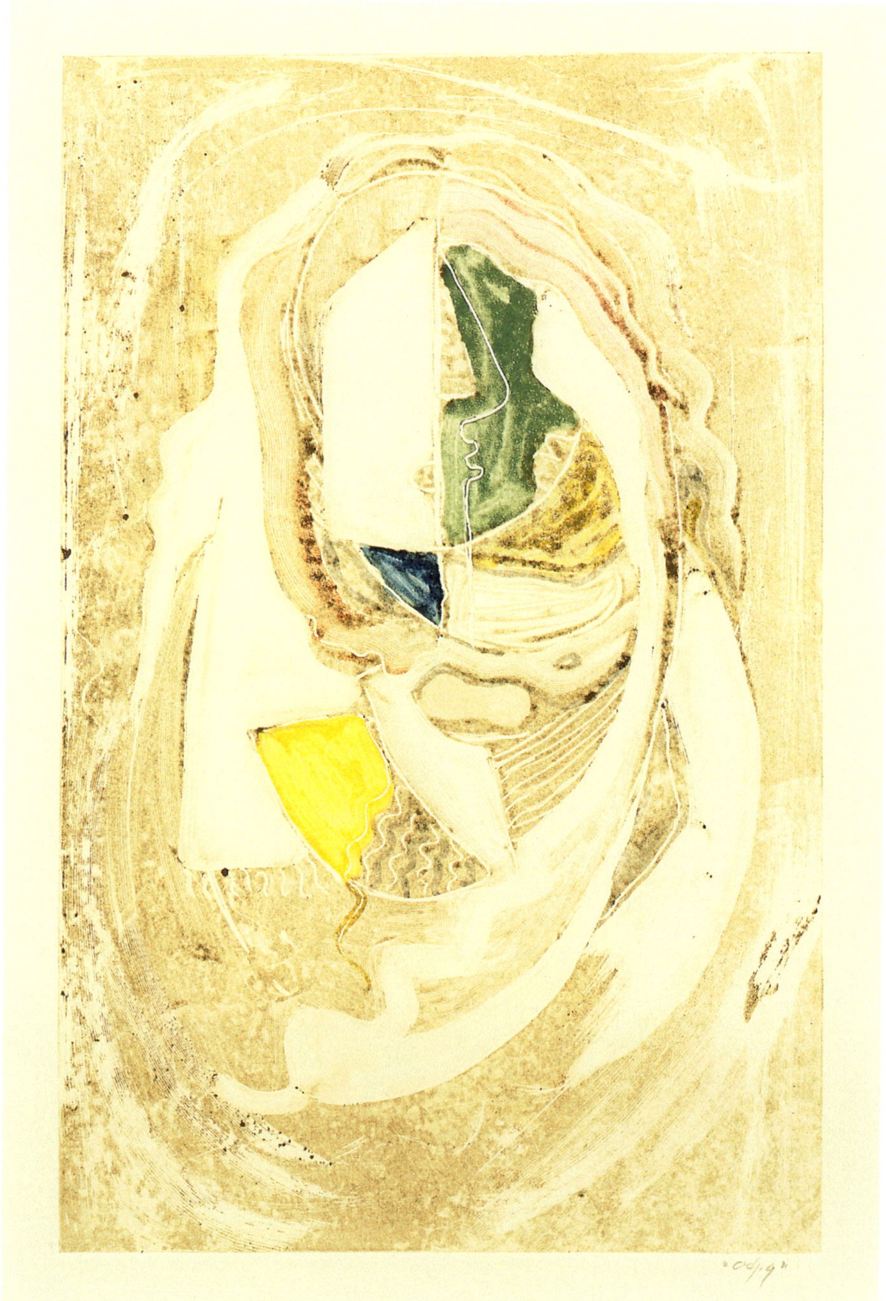

No title, 1982
monotype on paper
47 × 30 cm
Collection of Stan Somerville

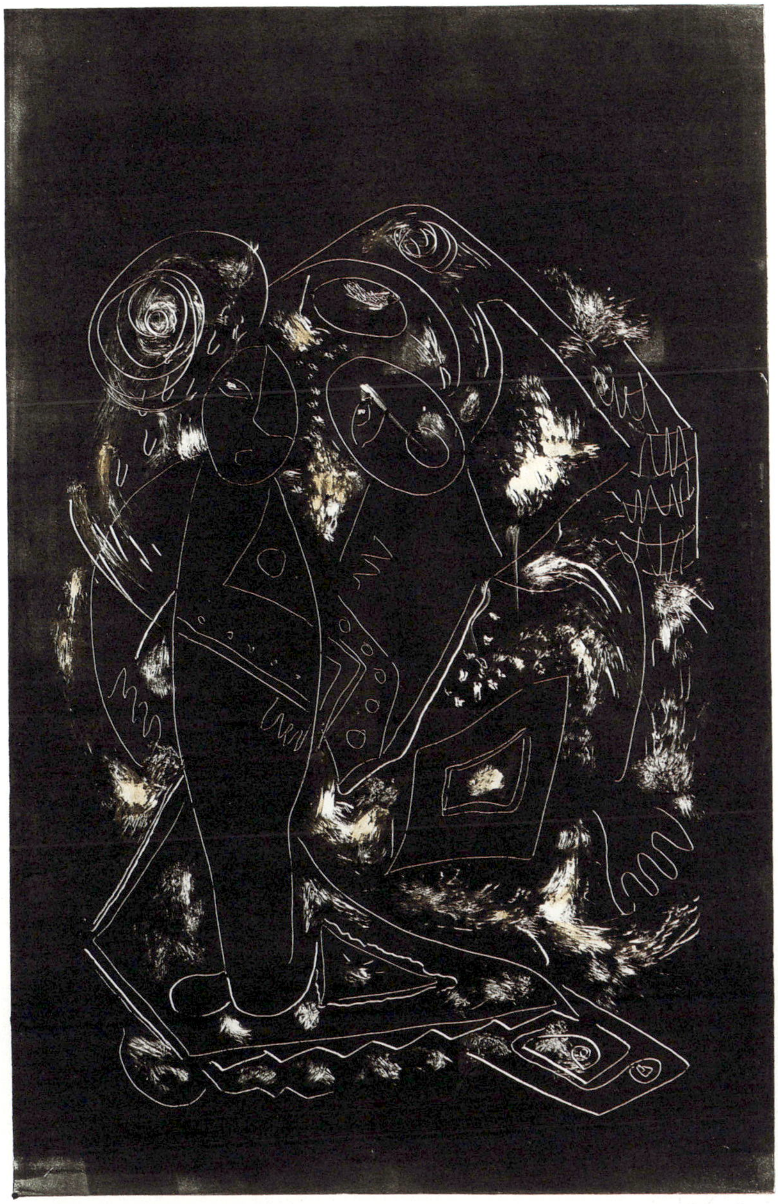

No title, 1982
monotype on paper
46 .5 × 30 cm
Collection of Stan Somerville

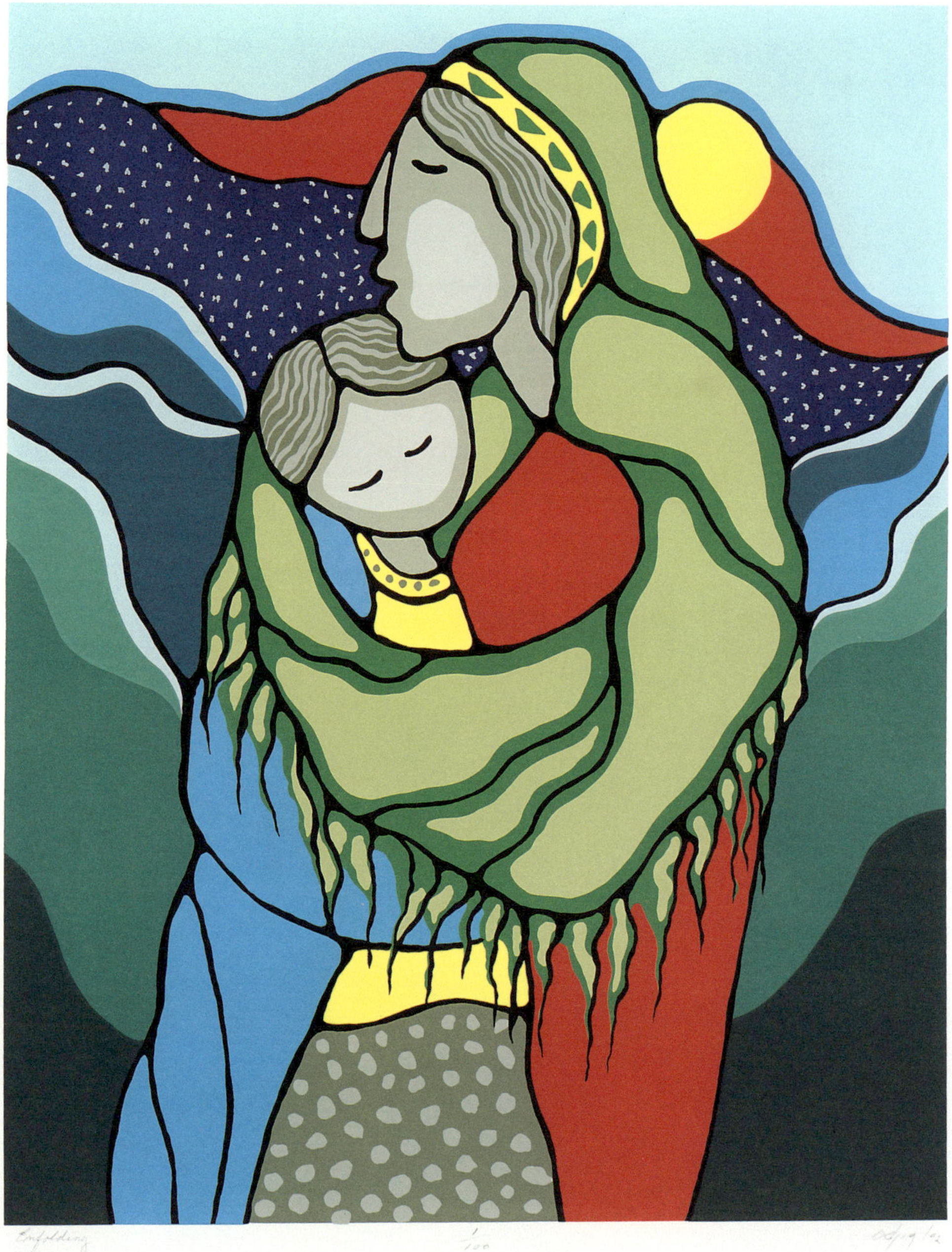

Enfolding, 1992
serigraph on paper, 1 / 100
53 × 42 cm
Kamloops Art Gallery Collection 1993-10
Kamloops Art Gallery Collecting Canadian Art Program

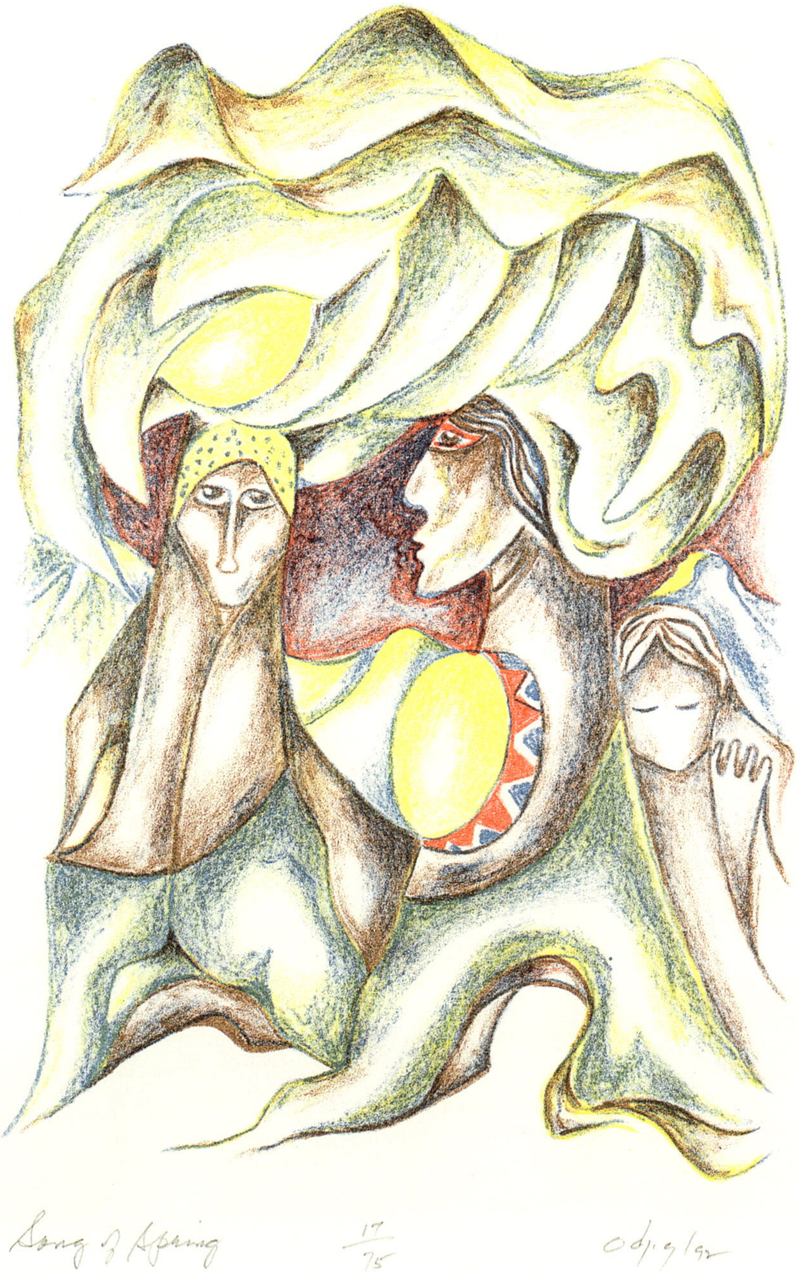

Song of Spring, 1992
lithograph on paper, 17/75
38 × 24 cm
Kamloops Art Gallery Collection 2004-013

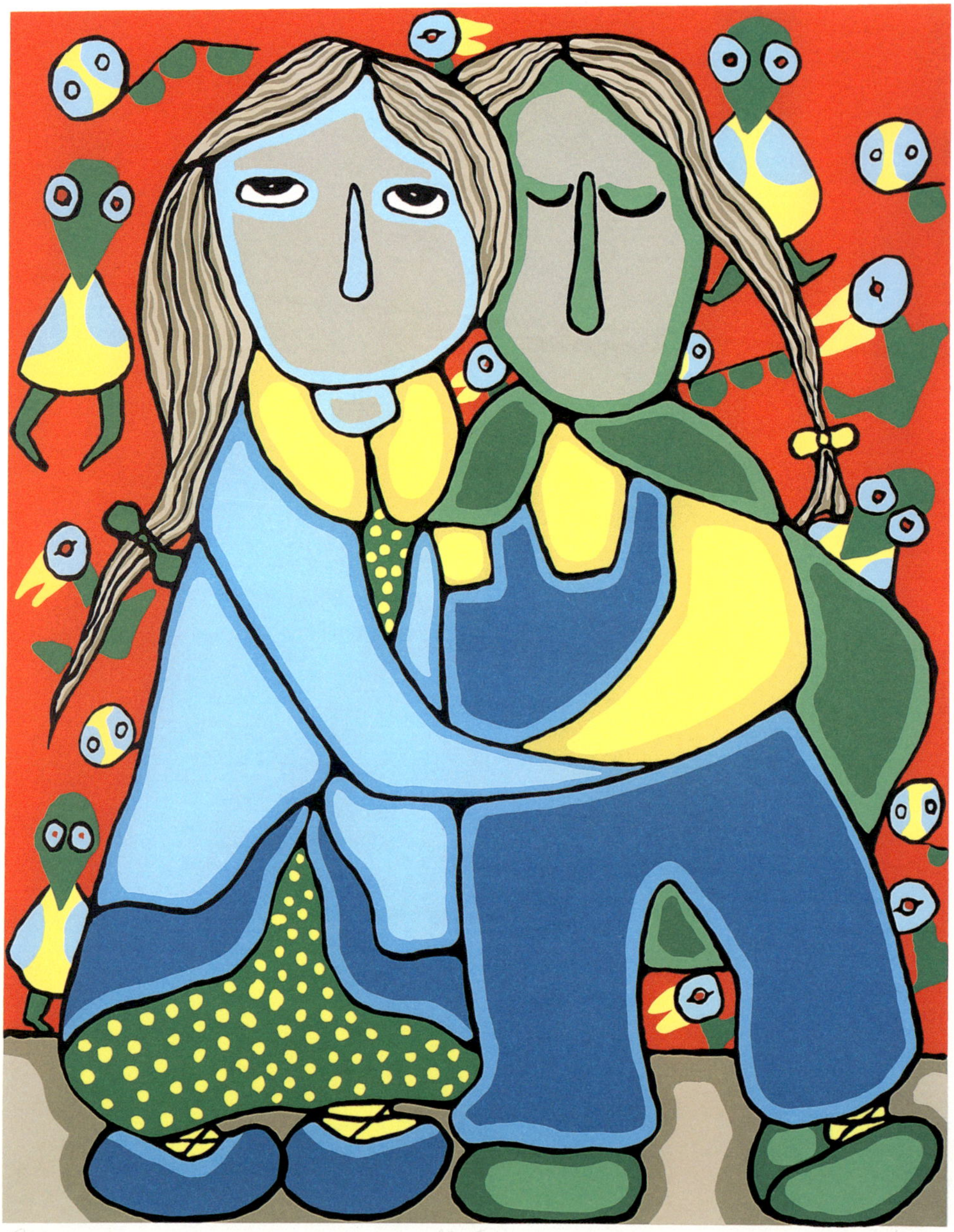

Memories, 1992
serigraph on paper, AP IV/X
52.5 × 40.8 cm
Collection of Stan Somerville

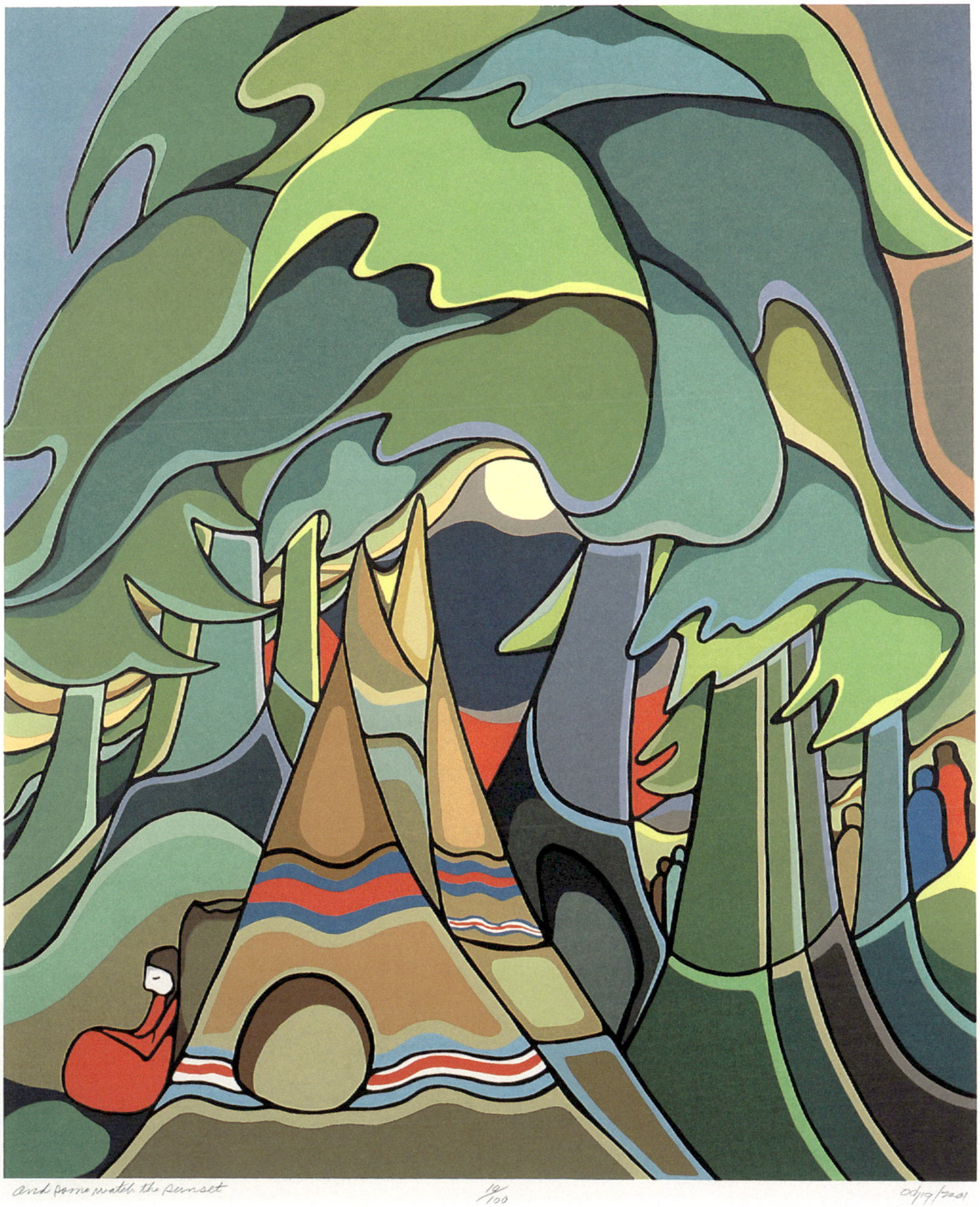

And Some Watch the Sunset, 2001
serigraph on paper, 10/100
73 × 60.8 cm
Kamloops Art Gallery Collection 2005-003

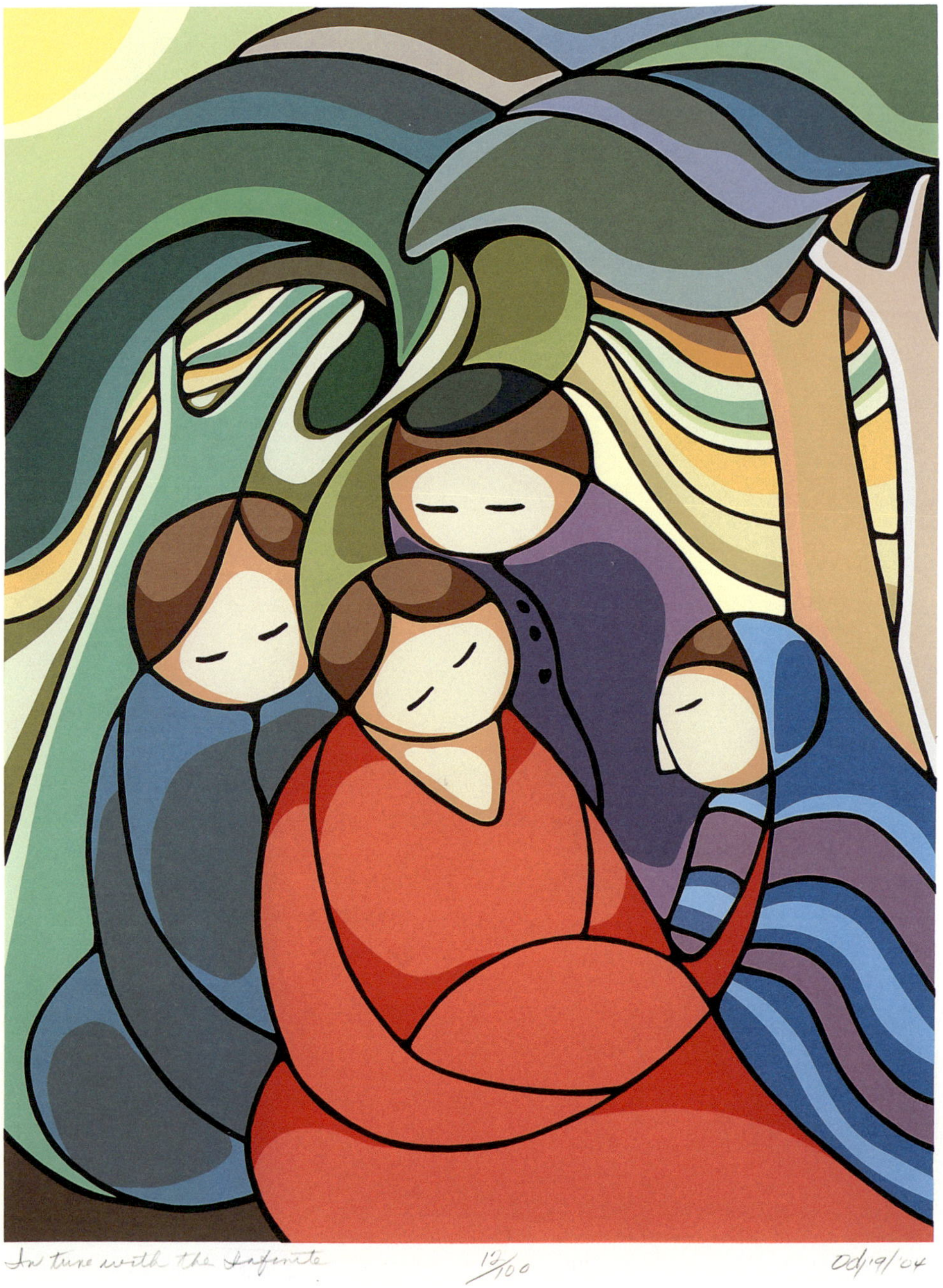

In Tune With the Infinite, 2004
serigraph on paper, 12/100
53.5 × 40.7 cm
Collection of Stan Somerville

If you destroy our legends
you also destroy our soul.

DAPHNE ODJIG

Wiseman, Eva, Article in *The Winnipeg Tribune*,
November 28, 1968

Prints in the Exhibition

Turtle Spirit, n.d.
print on paper, not editioned
23 × 11 cm
Canadian Museum of Civilization Collection

Untitled (The Eternal Conflict), 1968
serigraph on paper, not editioned
34.3 × 51.4 cm
Collection of The Winnipeg Art Gallery
Gift from the Estate of Arnold O. Brigden

Spirit of the Mighty Thunderbird, 1968
silkscreen on paper, not editioned
23 × 18 cm
Canadian Museum of Civilization Collection

Rolling Head, 1971
serigraph, 5/30
97.5 × 72 cm
Kamloops Art Gallery Collection 2003-073
Gift of Daphne Odjig

Nanabush and the Dancing Ducks, 1971?
ink (silkscreen) on paper, not editioned
24.6 × 24.6 cm
Canadian Museum of Civilization Collection

Thunderbird Woman, 1973
serigraph on paper, 13/48
71 × 55.5 cm
Kamloops Art Gallery Collection 2003-041
Purchased with the support of the Canada Council for the Arts Acquisition Assistance program, Ken Lepin, Elizabeth Illsey, and Linda and Manny Jules.

Indians Without Tipis, 1973
serigraph on paper, 39/50
49.5 × 65 cm
Collection of Stan Somerville

Hoop Dancer, 1974
serigraph on paper, 44/50
97.5 × 66 cm
Collection of Linda McMillan

Illustrations for *Tales from the Smokehouse*

Medicine Dream, 1974
serigraph on paper, 5/60
83 × 53.5 cm
Kamloops Art Gallery Collection 2003-039
Purchased with the support of the Canada Council for the Arts Acquisition Assistance program, Ken Lepin, Elizabeth Illsey, and Linda and Manny Jules.

Bad Medicine Woman, 1974
serigraph on paper, 33/60
87 × 50 cm
Kamloops Art Gallery Collection 2003-040
Purchased with the support of the Canada Council for the Arts Acquisition Assistance program, Ken Lepin, Elizabeth Illsey, and Linda and Manny Jules.

Nanabojou and His Daughter, 1975
serigraph on paper, 11/60
97 × 62 cm
Kamloops Art Gallery Collection 2003-038
Purchased with the support of the Canada Council for the Arts Acquisition Assistance program, Ken Lepin, Elizabeth Illsey, and Linda and Manny Jules.

The Squaw Man, 1975
serigraph on paper, 8/60
93 × 70 cm
Kamloops Art Gallery Collection 2003-042
Purchased with the support of the Canada Council for the Arts Acquisition Assistance program, Ken Lepin, Elizabeth Illsey, and Linda and Manny Jules.

The Evil Spell, 1975
serigraph on paper, AP
73.5 × 96.5 cm
Collection of Stan Somerville

Genesis, 1976
serigraph on paper, AP
73.5 × 61 cm
Collection of Daphne Odjig

Jerusalem Series

Western Wall — Jerusalem, 1976
serigraph on paper, 223/250
65.5 × 51.5 cm
Collection of Daphne Odjig

Spirit of Jerusalem, 1976
serigraph on paper, 11/250
63.5 × 51.5 cm
Collection of Stan Somerville

Jaffa Gate, 1976
serigraph on paper, 4/250
63.5 × 50.5 cm
Collection of Stan Somerville

Faiths of Jerusalem, 1976
serigraph on paper, 17/250
63.5 × 51 cm
Collection of Stan Somerville

Vision, 1976
serigraph on paper, AP
53 × 51 cm
Collection of Stan Somerville

Devotion, 1977
serigraph on paper, AP
25.5 × 25.5 cm
Kamloops Art Gallery Collection 2003-033
Purchased with the support of the Canada Council for the Arts Acquisition Assistance program, Ken Lepin, Elizabeth Illsey, and Linda and Manny Jules.

Arms of Security, 1977
serigraph on paper, AP
60.5 × 48 cm
Collection of Stan Somerville

Reflections, 1977
serigraph on paper, 39/98
29 × 22.9 cm
From the Simon Fraser University Collection

Visiting Grandma, 1977
serigraph on paper, AP
56 × 45.8 cm
Collection of Stan Somerville

Babysitter, 1977
serigraph on paper, AP
51 × 39.7 cm
Collection of Stan Somerville

Pow Wow Series

The Rhythm of the Drum, 1977
serigraph on paper, AP
60 × 50 cm
Kamloops Art Gallery Collection 2003-035
Purchased with the support of the Canada Council for the Arts Acquisition Assistance program, Ken Lepin, Elizabeth Illsey, and Linda and Manny Jules.

Fun Dance, 1977
serigraph on paper, AP
62 × 50 cm
Collection of Stan Somerville

Girl Hoop Dancer, 1977
serigraph on paper, AP
62 × 50.3 cm
Collection of Stan Somerville

Folk Singer, 1977
serigraph on paper, AP
61.8 × 50.1 cm
Collection of Stan Somerville

Eagle Dancer, 1977
serigraph on paper, AP
62 × 50.2 cm
Collection of Stan Somerville

Dominic and Lucy, 1977
serigraph on paper, AP
61.5 × 50 cm
Collection of Stan Somerville

Pow-Wow Singers, 1978
serigraph on paper, AP
50 × 40.4 cm
Kamloops Art Gallery Collection 2003-031
Purchased with the support of the Canada Council for the Arts Acquisition Assistance program, Ken Lepin, Elizabeth Illsey, and Linda and Manny Jules.

Devotion, 1978
serigraph on paper, AP
55 × 46 cm
Kamloops Art Gallery Collection 2003-036
Purchased with the support of the Canada Council for the Arts Acquisition Assistance program, Ken Lepin, Elizabeth Illsey, and Linda and Manny Jules.

Pow-Wow Dancer, 1978
serigraph on paper, AP
57.3 × 57.3 cm
Kamloops Art Gallery Collection 2003-037
Purchased with the support of the Canada Council for the Arts Acquisition Assistance program, Ken Lepin, Elizabeth Illsey, and Linda and Manny Jules.

Affection, 1978
serigraph on paper, AP
26.3 × 25.5 cm
Collection of Stan Somerville

Tribute to Courage, 1978
serigraph on paper, AP
57 × 46.5 cm
Collection of Stan Somerville

Indian Day School, 1978
serigraph on paper, AP
52 × 40.8 cm
Collection of Stan Somerville

Motherhood Series I

Chatting, 1979
serigraph on paper, III/125
34.5 × 25 cm
Kamloops Art Gallery Collection 2005-004

Companions, 1979
serigraph on paper, III/125
33.5 × 22 cm
Kamloops Art Gallery Collection 2005-005

New Friends, 1979
serigraph on paper, III/125
33.5 × 24.5 cm
Kamloops Art Gallery Collection 2005-006

Sharing, 1979
serigraph on paper, III/125
26 × 27.5 cm
Kamloops Art Gallery Collection 2005-007

Nanabush Loses His Eyeballs, 1979
print on paper, not editioned
14 × 11.5 cm
Canadian Museum of Civilization Collection

Spring, 1979
serigraph on paper, AP
53.5 × 46 cm
Collection of Daphne Odjig

Motherhood Series

Comforting, 1979
serigraph on paper, AP
27 × 23.5 cm
Collection of Daphne Odjig

First Parting, 1979
serigraph on paper, AP
25 × 21.3 cm
Collection of Daphne Odjig

Caring, 1979
serigraph on paper, AP
27 × 21.5 cm
Collection of Daphne Odjig

Getting His Wings, 1979
serigraph on paper, AP
27.5 × 21 cm
Collection of Daphne Odjig

Home Coming, 1979
serigraph on paper, AP
32 × 26 cm
Collection of Stan Somerville

Anthem, 1979
serigraph on paper, AP
32.5 × 26.7 cm
Collection of Stan Somerville

Pride, 1979
serigraph on paper, AP
55.5 × 45.5 cm
Collection of Stan Somerville

Together, 1979
serigraph on paper, AP
50 × 59.6 cm
Collection of Stan Somerville

In Prayer, 1980
serigraph on paper, AP
37 × 28 cm
Collection of Winnie Christian

Homage to Grandfather Series, dedicated to Jonas Odjig

Listening, 1980
serigraph on paper, AP
57 × 50.8 cm
Collection of Stan Somerville

Learning, 1980
serigraph on paper, AP
57 × 50.8 cm
Collection of Stan Somerville

Comforting, 1980
serigraph on paper, AP
57.5 × 51 cm
Collection of Stan Somerville

Belonging, 1980
serigraph on paper, AP
57.5 × 51 cm
Collection of Stan Somerville

Classmates, 1980
serigraph on paper, AP
36.5 × 28 cm
Collection of Stan Somerville

The Elders, 1981
serigraph on paper, APV/X
35.7 × 28 cm
Kamloops Art Gallery Collection 2003-034
Purchased with the support of the Canada Council for the Arts Acquisition Assistance program, Ken Lepin, Elizabeth Illsey, and Linda and Manny Jules.

Picking Flowers, 1981
serigraph on paper, 63/100
53.5 × 46.5 cm
Kamloops Art Gallery Collection 2005-008

Childhood Memories Series

Bath Time, 1981
serigraph on paper, AP VIII/XII
51.6 × 45.4 cm
Collection of Dave Barron

Piggyback, 1981
serigraph on paper, AP IX/XII
52 × 45.3 cm
Collection of Dave Barron

Fetching Water, 1981
serigraph on paper, AP IX/XII
52 × 45.3 cm
Collection of Dave Barron

Little Mothers, 1981
serigraph on paper, AP IX/XII
52.5 × 45.3 cm
Collection of Dave Barron

Donald's Outing, 1981
serigraph on paper, APm VII/XII
51 × 45.5 cm
Collection of Dave Barron

Playing School, 1981
serigraph on paper, AP IX/XII
52 × 45.3 cm
Collection of Dave Barron

Hide 'n Seek, 1981
serigraph on paper, AP VIII/XII
52 × 45.2 cm
Collection of Dave Barron

Husking Corn, 1981
serigraph on paper, AP IX/XII
52 × 45.5 cm
Collection of Dave Barron

Tree Climbing, 1981
serigraph on paper, AP IV/XII
52.5 × 45.5 cm
Collection of Dave Barron

Old Swimming Hole, 1981
serigraph on paper, AP IX/XII
52 × 45.4 cm
Collection of Dave Barron

Love Suite

Protection, 1981
serigraph on paper, AP
33.5 × 28 cm
Collection of Stan Somerville

Loving, 1981
serigraph on paper, AP
33 × 28 cm
Collection of Stan Somerville

Desire, 1981
serigraph on paper, AP
32 × 26.5 cm
Collection of Stan Somerville

Embracing, 1981
serigraph on paper, AP
32.5 × 27 cm
Collection of Stan Somerville

Day's End, 1982
serigraph on paper, 56/125
54.5 × 45.3 cm
Kamloops Art Gallery Collection 2005-001

With Granny, 1982
serigraph on paper, 25/125
54 × 45.3 cm
Kamloops Art Gallery Collection 2005-002

Mother's Embrace, 1982
ink (serigraph) on paper, AP XII/XII
53 × 46 cm
Canadian Museum of Civilization Collection

Bundled and Ready, 1982
serigraph on paper, AP VII/XII
54.5 × 45 cm
Collection of Stan Somerville

Monoprints

No title, 1982
monotype on paper
47 × 29.8 cm
Collection of Stan Somerville

No title, 1982
monotype on paper
47 × 30 cm
Collection of Stan Somerville

No title, 1982
monotype on paper
46 .5 × 30 cm
Collection of Stan Somerville

No title, 1982
monotype on paper
47 × 30 cm
Collection of Stan Somerville

Prayer Series

Praying with Grandma, 1983
serigraph on paper, AP III/XIII
31 × 25 cm
Collection of Daphne Odjig

Morning Prayer, 1983
serigraph on paper, AP VI/XIII
28 × 26 cm
Collection of Daphne Odjig

Gathering In Prayer, 1983
serigraph on paper, AP V/XII
28 × 25.5 cm
Collection of Stan Somerville

Evening Prayer, 1983
serigraph on paper, AP III/XIII
30.5 × 26 cm
Collection of Stan Somerville

Worship, 1983
serigraph on paper, 96/99
37.2 × 28 cm
Collection of Stan Somerville

Enfolding, 1992
serigraph on paper, 1/100
53 × 42 cm
Kamloops Art Gallery Collection 1993-10
Kamloops Art Gallery Collecting Canadian Art Program.

Life in Harmony, 1992
lithograph on paper, 17/75
37 × 23.5 cm
Kamloops Art Gallery Collection 2004-012

Song of Spring, 1992
lithograph on paper, 17/75
38 × 24 cm
Kamloops Art Gallery Collection 2004-013

Love Series

New Love, 1992
serigraph, 76/100
52.5 × 40.8 cm
Kamloops Art Gallery Collecion 2004-011

Awakening, 1992
serigraph on paper, AP III/X
52.5 × 40.8 cm
Collection of Stan Somerville

Companions, 1992
serigraph on paper, AP III/X
52.5 × 40.8 cm
Collection of Stan Somerville

Memories, 1992
serigraph on paper, AP IV/X
52.5 × 40.8 cm
Collection of Stan Somerville

And Some Watch the Sunset, 2001
serigraph on paper, 10/100
73 × 60.8 cm
Kamloops Art Gallery Collection 2005-003

Genesis, 2002
Commissioned by Canada Post
Pane of 24 Canadian 48¢ postage stamps
7 colour lithograph on gummed paper, matte varnish
24 × 19.3 cm
Kamloops Art Gallery Collection 2003-030
Gift of Linda Jules

In Tune With the Infinite, 2004
serigraph on paper, 12/100
53.5 × 40.7 cm
Collection of Stan Somerville

Daphne Odjig, R.C.A

b. Wikwemikong Reserve,
Manitoulin Island, Ontario, 1919

Solo Exhibitions

2005 *Daphne Odjig: Four Decades of Prints*, Kamloops Art Gallery, Kamloops, British Columbia

Celebration of Life, Hampton Gallery, Kamloops, British Columbia

2003 Book signing and exhibition, Hambleton Galleries, Kelowna, British Columbia

Hampton Gallery, Kamloops, British Columbia

2001 Book launch and exhibition, *Art of Daphne Odjig*, Gallery Gevik, Toronto, Ontario, Bear Claw Gallery, Edmonton, Alberta, and Hampton Gallery, Kamloops, British Columbia

1999 80th Birthday Celebration and Mini-Retrospective, Gallery Gevik, Toronto, Ontario

1998 *Daphne Odjig, A Retrospective* 1960–1998, Gallery Gevik, Toronto, Ontario

Retrospective Exhibition, Hampton Gallery, Kamloops, British Columbia

1997 Bear Claw Gallery, Edmonton, Alberta

Hampton Gallery, Kamloops, British Columbia

1996 Hampton Gallery, Kamloops, British Columbia

Gallery Gevik, Toronto, Ontario

1995 Gallery Phillip, Toronto, Ontario

Hambleton Galleries, Kelowna, British Columbia

1993 Book signing and exhibition, Hambleton Galleries, Kelowna, British Columbia, Bear Claw Gallery, Edmonton, Alberta, and Wallace Galleries Ltd., Calgary, Alberta

1992 Book launch for *A Paintbrush in my Hand*, Arts & Letters Club, Toronto, Ontario

Book signing and exhibition, Shayne Gallery, Montreal

Book signing and exhibition, Assiniboia Gallery, Regina, Saskatchewan

1991 Hambleton Galleries, Kelowna, British Columbia

1990 Shayne Gallery, Montreal, Quebec

Hambleton Galleries, Kelowna, British Columbia

1989 Robertson Gallery, Ottawa, Ontario

Gallery Phillip, Toronto, Ontario

1988 Shayne Gallery, Montreal, Quebec

1986 Gallery Phillip, Toronto, Ontario

1985 *Daphne Odjig, A Retrospective* 1946–1985, organized and circulated by the Thunder Bay National Exhibition Centre & Centre for Indian Art. Also exhibited at the McMichael Canadian Collection, Kleinberg, Ontario; the Woodland Indian Cultural Centre, Brantford, Ontario; and Laurentian University, Sudbury, Ontario

Robertson Gallery, Ottawa, Ontario

Shayne Gallery, Montreal, Quebec

1984 Gallery Phillip, Toronto, Ontario

1983 Shayne Gallery, Montreal, Quebec

1982 Robertson Gallery, Ottawa, Ontario

Assiniboia Gallery, Regina, Saskatchewan

Gold Design Fine Arts, Calgary, Alberta

1981 *Childhood Memories*, Children of the Raven Gallery, Vancouver, British Columbia

Shayne Gallery, Montreal, Quebec

1980 Children of the Raven Gallery, Vancouver, British Columbia

Parallels with Nature, Assiniboia Gallery, Regina, Saskatchewan

Behind the Mask, Robertson Gallery, Ottawa, Ontario

1979 Pollock Gallery, Toronto, Ontario

Time Passages, Gallery West, Vancouver, British Columbia

1977 Wah-sa Gallery, Winnipeg, Manitoba

Images for a Canadian Heritage, Vancouver, British Columbia

Lefebre Gallery, Edmonton, Alberta

1976 *Jerusalem Series*, Bashford & Schwarz Gallery, Calgary, Alberta

1974 New Warehouse Gallery of Native Art, Winnipeg, Manitoba

1971 Smotra Folklore Festival, Yugoslavia

1970 International Peace Garden, Manitoba/North Dakota

1969 Viscount Gort Motor Hotel, Winnipeg, Manitoba

1968 Brandon University, Brandon, Manitoba

1967 Lakehead Art Centre, Port Arthur, Ontario

Group Exhibitions

2001 *The Helen Band Collection*, Thunder Bay Art Gallery, Thunder Bay, Ontario

2000 *Exposed: Aesthetics of Aboriginal Erotic Art*, Ottawa, Ontario

First Nations Exposition, Wheteng Gallery, Curve Lake, Ontario

Hampton Gallery, Kamloops, British Columbia

1999 *Exposed: Aesthetics of Aboriginal Erotic Art*, curated by Lee Ann Martin and Morgan Wood, MacKenzie Art Gallery, Regina, Saskatchewan

1998 Hampton Gallery, Kamloops, British Columbia

1997 *A Celebration of the Art of Canada, First People at Rideau Hall*, Indian Art Centre, Department of Indian and Northern Affairs, Gatineau, Quebec

Hampton Gallery, Kamloops, British Columbia

1996 Hampton Gallery, Kamloops, British Columbia

1995 *Voices of Vision – Resurgence*, En-owkin Centre & Art Gallery of the South Okanagan, Penticton, British Columbia

1992–93 *Canada's First People, a Celebration of Contemporary Native Visual Arts*, touring Canada and Tokyo, Japan. Sponsored by Syncrude Canada Ltd.

1989 *Woodlands: Contemporary Art of the Anishnabe*, Thunder Bay National Exhibition Centre and Centre for Indian Art, Thunder Bay, Ontario

1988 *An Exhibition of Contemporary Native Art*, Joseph D. Carrier Art Gallery, Toronto, Ontario

1987 *The Los Angeles Celebration of Contemporary Native Art*, Southwest Museum, Los Angeles, California

Manitoulin Island – The Third Layer, Thunder Bay Art Gallery, Thunder Bay, Ontario

1986 *Ascending Culture*, Les Terrasses de la Chaudière, Hull, Quebec

New Beginnings, Native Business Summit, Toronto, Ontario

Keepers of Our Culture, Woodland Indian Cultural Educational Centre, Brantford, Ontario

Artists of Northeastern Ontario, Ontario North Now, Toronto, Ontario

1985 *Challenges*, Meervaart Cultural Centre, Holland Festival, Amsterdam, Holland

Two Worlds, Mackenzie Art Gallery, Regina, Saskatchewan

The Best of Our Collections, in the Spirit of Sharing, Woodland Indian Cultural Educational Centre, Brantford, Ontario

Indian and Eskimo Art Canada, Holland Festival, Amsterdam, sponsored by the National Museum of Man, Ottawa, Ontario

1984 *Norval Morriseau and The Emergence of The Image Makers*, Art Gallery of Ontario, Toronto, Ontario

1983 *Contemporary Indian and Inuit Art of Canada*, Department of Indian Affairs and Northern Development, Ottawa, for the United Nations Building, New York City, New York. Touring: Organization of American States; Duke University, Durham, North Carolina; The Hall of State, Dallas, Texas; The Southwest Museum, Los Angeles, California

Contemporary Indian Art at Rideau Hall, Department of Indian Affairs and Northern Development, Ottawa, Ontario

1982 *Renewal: Masterworks of Contemporary Indian Art from the National Museum of Man*, organized by the Thunder Bay National Exhibition Centre and Centre for Indian Art, Thunder Bay, Ontario

The Indian Individualist Show, joint project of the Assiniboia Gallery, The World Assembly of First Nations, and the Saskatchewan Indian Federated College, Regina, Saskatchewan

Wandering Spirits: Contemporary Native Artists and Their Art, Windsong Galleries, Mississauga, Ontario

1981 Rothman's Gallery, Sudbury, Ontario

Traditions & Change, touring: Sub Theatre, Edmonton Centre, Edmonton, Alberta

1979 Glenhyrst Gallery, Brantford, Ontario

Woodland Indian Cultural Educational Centre, Brantford, Ontario

1978 *One Hundred Years of Native American Painting*, Oklahoma Museum of Art, Oklahoma

Eagle Down Gallery, Edmonton, Alberta

1977 *Links to a Tradition*, Department of Indian Affairs and Northern Development, for travel to centres in Brazil

Contemporary Indian Arts: The Trail from the Past to the Future, Mackenzie Gallery, Regina, Saskatchewan; Trent University, Peterborough, Ontario

Modern Native Canadian Art, Hart House Art Gallery, University of Toronto, Toronto, Ontario

Kinsmen Centre, Calgary, Alberta

1976 Laurentian University, Sudbury, Ontario

From Women's Eyes: Women Painters in Canada, Agnes Etherington Art Centre, Queens University, Kingston, Ontario

Etobicoke Civic Centre, Etobicoke, Ontario

Janet Ian Cameron Gallery, University of Manitoba, Winnipeg, Manitoba

Indian Art '76, Woodland Indian Cultural Educational Centre, Brantford, Ontario

Contemporary Native Art of Canada: The Woodland Indians, Royal Ontario Museum, Toronto, Ontario; Canada House Art Gallery, London, England; Aula Luisen Schule, Lahr, Germany

1975 Winnipeg Art Gallery, Winnipeg, Manitoba

Native Arts Festival, Niagara-on-the-Lake, Ontario

Dominion Gallery, Montreal, Quebec

Wallack Gallery, Ottawa, Ontario

Art Emporium, Vancouver, British Columbia

Indian Art '75, Woodland Indian Cultural Educational Centre, Brantford, Ontario

Winnipeg Inn, Winnipeg, Manitoba

1974 Janet Ian Cameron Gallery, University of Manitoba, Winnipeg, Manitoba

Oakville Centennial Gallery, Oakville, Ontario

New Warehouse Gallery, Winnipeg, Manitoba

Canadian Indian Art '74, Royal Ontario Museum, Toronto, Ontario

1973 *Nee Chee*, T. Eaton Co., Winnipeg, Manitoba

Professional Native Indian Artists, Gallery Anthropos, London, England

1972 *Treaty Numbers 23, 287, 1171*, Winnipeg Art Gallery, Winnipeg, Manitoba

1971 L'Agence de co-opération culturelle et technique, Canada, France, Belgium

1970 Minot State University, North Dakota

Canadian Guild of Crafts, Montreal, Quebec

Canadian Pavilion, Expo '70, Osaka, Japan

1964 Wikwemikong Manitoulin Island National Indian Council, 110 paintings by various artists purchased by Indian Affairs.

Commissions

2002 *Genesis*, postage stamp, Canada Post

1996 *Enfolding*, limited edition print portfolio Kamloops Art Gallery, Kamloops, British Columbia

1986 *Tomorrow Will Hold Our Past* and *We Dance Through Time*, diptych painting, Glenview Corporation, Ottawa, Ontario

1984 *Spiritual Renewal*, painting, Laurentian University Museum and Art Centre, Sudbury, Ontario

1978 *The Indian in Transition*, mural, National Museum of Man, Ottawa, Ontario, now the Canadian Museum of Civilization, Gatineau, Quebec.

1975 *Jerusalem Series*, El Al (Israel Airlines)

1973 *From Mother Earth Flows the River of Life*, painting, Royal Ontario Museum, Toronto, Ontario

1972 *Creation of the World*, mural, Manitoba Museum of Man and Nature, Winnipeg, Manitoba

1971 *Creation of the World*, mural, Peguis High School, Hodgson, Manitoba

1970 *Earth Mother*, Expo '70 in Osaka, Japan

Awards

2003 XPression Awards, initiative of National Film Board of Canada championing cultural diversity

2002 Doctor of Letters, Conferred by Okanagan University College, Kelowna, British Columbia

Commemorative Golden Jubilee Medal (Queen Elizabeth II)

1998 National Aboriginal Achievement Award, Toronto, Ontario

1996 Doctor of Education, *honoris causa*, conferred by Nipissing University of North Bay, Ontario

Honorary Patron of the Ojibway Cultural Foundation Capital campaign, West Bay, Ontario

1994 Presented Certificate of Honour by the En'owkin Centre, Penticton, British Columbia and Canada's Drug Strategy Program

1993 Presented Eagle Feather by SCANA (Society of Canadian Artists of Native Ancestry) at the 5th National Native Symposium, Halifax, Nova Scotia

1992 Commemorative Medal for the 125th Anniversary of the Confederation of Canada

1989 Elected to the Royal Canadian Academy of Art

1988–93 Honorary Board Member of the Canadian Heritage Foundation

1986 Appointed to the Order of Canada, C.M., investiture in 1987

1985 Doctor of Law, *honoris causa*, conferred by the University of Toronto

1982 Doctor of Letters, *honoris causa*, conferred by Laurentian University, Sudbury

1978 Presented Eagle Feather by Chief Wakageshig on behalf of the Wikwemikong Reserve, in recognition of artistic accomplishments. This honour was previously reserved for men to acknowledge prowess in hunt or war.

1977 Canada Silver Jubilee Medal

1973 Swedish Brucebo Foundation Scholarship and resident artist at the Brucebo Foundation studio, Visby, Island of Gotland, Sweden

Manitoba Arts Council Bursary

1971 Arts Grant for tour and exhibition of painting at the Smotra Folklore Festival, Yugoslavia

1963 Member of the British Columbia Federation of Artists

Collections

Ameco Canadian Petroleum Ltd, Calgary, Alberta

Art Gallery of Ontario, Toronto, Ontario

ATS Aerospace Inc., St. Bruno, Quebec

Brandon University, Brandon, Manitoba

Canada Council Art Bank, Ottawa, Ontario

Canadian Museum of Civilization, Gatineau, Quebec

Department of Indian Affairs and Northern Development, Ottawa, Ontario

Department of Indian Affairs, Winnipeg, Manitoba

Glenbow Foundation, Calgary, Alberta

Glenview Corporation, Ottawa, Ontario

Government of Israel, Jerusalem

Government of Newfoundland, St John's, Newfoundland

Government of Ontario, Sudbury, Ontario

Gulf Canada Resources Ltd., Calgary, Alberta

The Helen Band Collection, Toronto, Ontario

Hospital for Sick Children, Toronto, Ontario

Kamloops Art Gallery, Kamloops, British Columbia

Laurentian University Museum and Art Centre, Sudbury, Ontario

MacKenzie Art Gallery, Regina, Saskatchewan

Manitoba Centennial Centre Corp., Winnipeg, Manitoba

Manitoba Government, Winnipeg, Manitoba

Manitoba Indian Brotherhood, Winnipeg, Manitoba

Manitoba Museum of Man and Nature, Winnipeg, Manitoba

McMichael Canadian Collection, Kleinburg, Ontario

National Gallery of Canada, Ottawa, Ontario

New College, University of Toronto, Toronto, Ontario

Norce Energy Ltd. Calgary, Alberta

Nova Corporation, Calgary, Alberta

Ojibwe Cultural Foundation, West Bay, Manitoulin Island, Ontario

Peguis High School, Hodgson, Manitoba

Pontiac School, Wikwemikong, Ontario

Princess Margaret Hospital, Toronto, Ontario

Prudential Assurance Co. Ltd., Toronto, Ontario

Reader's Digest, Montreal, Quebec

Salmon Arm Savings and Credit Union, Salmon Arm, British Columbia

Sir Wilfrid Laurier University, Waterloo, Ontario

Thunder Bay National Exhibition Centre and Centre for Indian Art, Thunder Bay, Ontario

Tom Thomson Gallery, Owen Sound, Ontario

Winnipeg Art Gallery, Manitoba

Woodland Indian Cultural Educational Centre, Brantford, Ontario

Related Employment and Activities

1998 Guest Speaker, Wikwemikong Graduation Ceremony.

1997 Juror, Okanagan Mainline Regional Arts Council

1996 Guest Speaker, 20th Anniversary Celebration of the Thunder Bay Art Gallery, Thunder Bay, Ontario

Juror for Canadian Native Arts Foundation grants and Scholarships Application, Toronto, Ontario

1995 Juror for work for Indian Affairs, Ottawa, Ontario

Advisory Committee Member for the Canadian National Committee for Jerusalem 3000

1993 Opened Retrospective Exhibition of the late Jackson Beardy: *Jackson Beardy: A Life's Work*, organized and circulated by Winnipeg Art Gallery, Manitoba

Lansdowne Scholar & Discourse, "Arts in Education," The Lansdowne Lectures, University of Victoria, British Columbia

Keynote Speaker, The B.C. Art Teachers' 37th Annual Conference, "Art Reflecting Cultures," Kelowna, British Columbia

1986 Board Member of the Canadian Native Arts Foundation

1974 Warehouse Gallery, Winnipeg, Manitoba: Owner, Manager

1973 Co-Founder of Professional Native Indian Artists Inc.

1971 Arts Instructor at Manitou Arts Foundation, Schreiber Island, Ontario

1970 Indian Prints of Canada Ltd.: Founder, President

Films and Documentaries

2003 *The Life and Work of the Woodland Artists*, First Voice Multimedia Inc.

2003 XPression award video (initiative of the National Film Board of Canada)

1989 *Window on Canada, Daphne Odjig, Painter*, Tokyo Television, Japan

1981 *Spirits Speaking Through*, Spectrum CBC, Canada

1976 *Three Artists, Three Styles*, Henning Jacobson Productions

1973 *Colours of Pride*, National Film Board, Canada

Selected Publications, Bibliography, References

Bayer, Fern. *The Ontario Collection*. Markham, Ontario: Fitzhenry & Whiteside for the Ontario Heritage Foundation, 1984.

Blundell, Valda, and Ruth Phillips. "If it's not shamanic, is it sham? An examination of media responses to Woodland School art." *Anthropologica* 25 (1983): 117-32.

Boyer, Bob, and Lee-Ann Martin. *The Powwow: An Art History*. Regina: MacKenzie Art Gallery, 2000.

Bringhurst, Robert, Geoffrey James, Russell Keziere and Doris Shadboldt, ed's. *Visions: Contemporary Art in Canada*. Vancouver/Toronto: Douglas & McIntyre, 1983.

Canada's First People: A Celebration of Contemporary Canadian Visual Arts. Fort McMurray, Alberta: Syncrude Canada Ltd., 1992.

A Celebration of Contemporary Canadian Native Art. Los Angeles: Southwestern Museum, 1987.

Cinader, Bernard. *Contemporary Indian Art – The Trail from the Past to the Future*. Peterborough, Ontario: MacKenzie Gallery and Native Studies Program, Trent University, 1977.

____________. *Woodlands: Contemporary Art of the Anishnabe*. Thunder Bay, Ontario: Thunder Bay Art Gallery, 1989.

Dolan, Marlena. *Just Talking About Ourselves*. Penticton, B.C.: Theytus Books Ltd., 1994.

Duffek, Karen, and Tom Hill. *Beyond History*. Vancouver: Vancouver Art Gallery, 1989.

Freedman, Adele. "Reservations are for Artists: Liberating the Native Imagination with Daphne Odjig." *Toronto Life*, June 1979.

Fry, Jacqueline. *Treaty Numbers 23, 287, 1171, Three Indian Painters of the Prairies*. Winnipeg Art Gallery, Winnipeg, Manitoba, 1972.

____________. "Treaty Numbers 23, 287, 1171", *Arts Canada*, Autumn 1972.

Hill, Tom. "Canadian Indian Art – Its Death & Rebirth." *Art Magazine*, Summer 1974.

Hoffman, Gerhard, ed. *In the Shadow of the Sun: Essays by Gerald McMaster et al.* Hull, Quebec: Canadian Museum of Civilization, 1988.

Houle, Robert. "Odjig: An Artist's Transition." *The Native Perspective*, 3 no. 2 (1979).

____________. *New Work by a New Generation*. Regina: Mackenzie Art Gallery, 1982.

Houle, Robert, Diana Nemiroff, and Charlotte Townsend-Gault. *Land, Spirit, Power*. Ottawa: National Gallery of Canada, 1992.

Hume, Christopher. "The New Age of Indian Art." *Maclean's*, 22 January 1979.

Knapp, Millie. "Daphne Odjig, Inspired by Nature." *Aboriginal Voices*, no. 5 (1998).

Lang, Andrea. "Odjig." *Westworld*, Jan.-Feb. 1979.

Logie, Pat Richardson. *Chronicles of Pride*. Calgary: Detselig Enterprises Ltd., 1990.

Martin, Elizabeth, and Vivian Meye. *Female Gazes: Seventy-five Women Artists*. Toronto: Second Story Press, 1977.

Matuz, Roger, ed. *St. James Guide to Native North American Artists*. Detroit: St. James Press, 1998.

McLuhan, Elizabeth, and Tom Hill. *Norval Morriseau and the Emergence of the Image Makers – Daphne Odjig: Innovator and Pioneer*. Toronto: Art Gallery of Ontario, 1984.

McLuhan, Elizabeth, and Roz M. Vanderburgh. *Daphne Odjig: A Retrospective* 1946–1985. Thunder Bay, Ontario: Thunder Bay National Exhibition Centre & Centre for Indian Art, 1985.

________________. *Daphne Odjig: A Retrospective* 1946–1985. Thunder Bay, Ontario: Thunder Bay Art Gallery, 1985.

McMaster, Gerald et al. *In the Shadow of the Sun: Perspectives on Contemporary Native Art*. Hull, Quebec: Canadian Museum of Civilization, 1993.

Newlands, Anne. *Canadian Art: From its Beginnings to 2000*. Willowdale, Ontario: Firefly Books, 2000.

Odjig, Daphne. *The Nanabush Series* [ten children's books written and illustrated by Daphne Odjig]. Toronto: Ginn & Co., 1971.

Podedworny, Carol. *Woodlands: Contemporary Art of the Anishnabe*. Thunder Bay, Ontario: Thunder Bay Art Gallery, 1989.

Pringle, Heather. "Spirits Journey: The Life and Art of Daphne Odjig." *Equinox*, July/August 1986.

Scale, Alexander, ed. *Treasures of Canada*. Toronto: Samuel-Stevens, 1980.

Schwartz, Herbert. "Daphne Odjig." *ArtsWest*, no. 2 (1977)

Schwartz, Herbert, illustrated by Daphne Odjig. *Tales from the Smokehouse*. Edmonton: Hurtig Publishers, 1974.

Southcott, Beth. *The Sound of the Drum*. Erin, Ontario: Boston Mills Press, 1984.

Tan-William, Conchita, and Shieu Loon Kong. *Canadian Achievers and their Mentors*. Prime Mentors of Canada. Toronto: University of Toronto Press, 1994.

Vanderburgh. R.M., and M.E. Southcott. *A Paintbrush in My Hand*. Toronto: Natural Heritage/Natural History Inc., 1992.

Vedan, Barbara. "The Daphne Odjig Mural: *The Indian in Transition*." *ArtsWest*, 3 no. 6 (1978).

Warner, John Anson. "Contemporary Algonkin Legend Painters." *American Indian Art Magazine* (1978).

________________. "Daphne Odjig: traditional elements combined with surrealistic influences." *Native Arts/West* 1, no. 7 (1981): 26-29.

________________. "New Visions in Canadian Plains Painting." *American Indian Art Magazine*, 10 (Spring 1985): 46-53.

Woodley, Barbara. *Portraits: Canadian Women in Focus*. Toronto: Doubleday Canada Ltd., 1983.

Zuk, Dr. W.M., and Dr. D.L. Berland. *Art: First Nations: Tradition And Innovation*. Montreal: Art Image Publications Inc., 1992.

A catalogue of the exhibition
Daphne Odjig: Four Decades of Prints held at
Kamloops Art Gallery
May 29 to August 21, 2005,
curated by Jann LM Bailey.

TOURING TO
The Winnipeg Art Gallery
22 April to 16 July 2006

Canadian Museum of Civilization
Opening 11 October 2007

Art Gallery of Hamilton
21 September 2008 to 5 January 2009

First printing 2005. Redesigned and reprinted 2006.

PUBLISHED BY KAMLOOPS ART GALLERY
101 – 465 Victoria Street, Kamloops, British Columbia
Canada V2C 2A9
TELEPHONE 250.377.2400
FACSIMILE 250.828.0662
E-MAIL kamloopsartgallery@kag.bc.ca
WEBSITE www.kag.bc.ca

CATALOGUE COORDINATOR Erin Moen
COPY EDITORS Jen Budney, Trish Keegan
PHOTOGRAPHY Victor Hamm,
except p. 25, Ernest Mayer, The Winnipeg Art Gallery
CATALOGUE DESIGN hundreds & thousands

Distributed by ABC Art Books Canada
www.abcartbookscanada.com

Printed in Canada by Hemlock Printers

COVER IMAGE
Daphne Odjig
Together, 1979
serigraph
Collection of Stan Somerville

Library and Archives Canada Cataloguing in Publication

Odjig, Daphne, 1919 –

Daphne Odjig : four decades of prints / Foreword by Jann L.M. Bailey : essay by Morgan Wood

Catalogue of an exhibition held at the Kamloops Art Gallery, May 28 – Aug. 21 , 2005.

Includes bibliographical references.

ISBN 1-895497-62-0 (bound). – ISBN1-895497-61-2 (pbk.)

1. Odjig, Daphne, 1919 – --Exhibitions. I. Wood, Morgan II. Kamloops Art Gallery III. Title. IV. Title: Four decades of prints.

NE543.O34A4 2005 769.92
C2005902819-X

The Kamloops Art Gallery is a registered not-for-profit society. We gratefully acknowledge the financial support of City of Kamloops, Province of British Columbia through the British Columbia Arts Council, the Canada Council for the Arts, Department of Canadian Heritage through the Museums Assistance Program and Young Canada Works in Heritage Institutions, corporate donations and sponsorships, foundation grants, general donations and memberships.